Do

http.

SCAN ME

Table of Contents

Disclaimer

This biography book is a work of nonfiction based on the public life of a famous person. The author has used publicly available information to create this work. While the author has thoroughly researched the subject and attempted to depict it accurately, it is not meant to be an exhaustive study of the subject. The views expressed in this book are those of the author alone and do not necessarily reflect those of any organization associated with the subject. This book should not be taken as an endorsement, legal advice, or any other form of professional advice. This book was written for entertainment purposes only.

Introduction

Immerse yourself in the tumultuous and unprecedented political journey of Donald John Trump, the 45th President of the United States, in this comprehensive biography that captures the complexities and controversies surrounding his presidency. Born on June 14, 1946, Donald John Trump first made his name as a businessman, expanding his father's real estate business to include iconic skyscrapers, hotels and golf courses, all under the banner of the Trump Organization.

This meticulously documented book traces Trump's evolution from real estate mogul to media personality, before his unexpected political rise. With no military or government experience, Trump's victory in the 2016 presidential election marked a historic moment, accompanied by fervent support and opposition. The book looks at his populist, protectionist and nationalist policy positions, which sparked large-scale protests and debate.

As president, Trump's policies have left an indelible mark on the nation, from immigration measures and environmental rollbacks to tax cuts and Supreme Court appointments. The story explores his handling of world affairs, from trade wars with China to diplomatic engagements with North Korea. Unprecedented in American politics, Trump's presidency has been marked by conspiracy theories, controversial statements and a divisive approach that scholars and historians have ranked among the nation's most contentious.

Looking beyond his tenure, the book provides an insightful analysis of Trump's post-presidential activities, including legal challenges, impeachment proceedings and his enduring influence on the Republican Party. As Trump announces his bid for the 2024 presidential election against a backdrop of legal challenges, this biography offers a timely, in-depth exploration of a figure who continues to shape the political landscape.

Donald Trump

Donald Trump, born June 14, 1946 in New York City, is an American billionaire businessman, entertainer, television producer and statesman. A member of the Republican Party, he is the 45 President of the United States, from January 20, 2017 to January 20, 2021.

Son of real estate developer Fred Trump, he studied at the Wharton School (Pennsylvania). In 1971, he took over the family business, renaming it The Trump Organization. From then on, he built up an empire with prestigious buildings, such as Trump Tower, and properties abroad. The owner of casinos, luxury residences and golf courses, he also made numerous investments in other fields (sports, media, beauty contests, etc.).

A media celebrity since the 1980s, he has been heavily involved in television. From 2004 to 2015, he hosted the record-breaking reality show *The Apprentice,* in which he popularized the expression "You'*re fired!*

In politics, he joined the Republican Party in 1987, then the Reform Party for two years. After being a resolute opponent of Republican President George W. Bush, under whose presidency he joined the Democratic Party, he returned to the Republican Party in 2009. He criticizes the policies of Democratic President Barack Obama, and for several years repeated conspiratorial rumors about his citizenship.

While his campaign was initially not taken seriously by observers, he won the Republican Party's nomination in the 2016 presidential primaries. Presenting himself as an opponent of the *establishment* and political correctness, he uses a bellicose tone and multiplies controversial statements. In particular, he pledged to reduce immigration. His rhetoric was often described as populist, nationalist, protectionist and climate-skeptic. His victory in the presidential election over Democrat Hillary Clinton, who was nevertheless well ahead of him in the popular vote, thwarted almost all predictions.

During his term of office, he signed decrees restricting immigration - particularly from Muslim countries - extended the border wall with Mexico, withdrew his country from the Paris climate and Iran nuclear agreements, recognized Jerusalem as the capital of Israel, restored relations with North Korea, renegotiated NAFTA and CEUMTA, and oversaw the peace agreement between Israel and the United Arab Emirates. On the economic front, he reduced compulsory levies and all kinds of taxes more generally, launched a trade war targeting China in particular, and enjoyed positive results in terms of employment and growth until the health crisis of 2020.

His presidency was marked by the exceptional renewal of one-third of the highly influential US Supreme Court, to which he gave a very conservative tinge, and was regularly accused of maintaining an ambiguous stance towards violent far-right groups. His unusual style of governance - in particular, his offensive, Twitter-focused communication - is a frequent source of controversy, and he maintains an openly hostile relationship with the press, with the exception of certain conservative media outlets.

At the beginning of 2020, accused of abusing his power to pressure Ukrainian President Volodymyr Zelensky into providing information on his presidential rival Joe Biden, he underwent an initial impeachment procedure, following which he was acquitted by the Senate. Shortly afterwards, his handling of the Covid-19 pandemic was widely criticized, and during this period he withdrew the United States from the World Health Organization (WHO).

As a candidate in the 2020 presidential election, he was defeated by Joe Biden. Refusing to concede defeat, he filed legal appeals, almost all of which were rejected, and delayed the presidential transition. On January 6, 2021, the storming of the Capitol by some of his supporters, notably from the ultra-right, after he had given an inflammatory speech, was considered an insurrection or attempted coup d'état, and an episode of political violence unprecedented in an advanced democracy. Unprecedented for an American president, a second impeachment procedure was launched against him, again without success. He refused to attend his successor's inauguration.

Retaining significant influence within the Republican Party, he announced his candidacy for the 2024 presidential election in November 2022. At the same time, he faced numerous legal problems, notably for his role in the assault on the Capitol, his attempts to reverse the outcome of the 2020 presidential election, and various accusations of corruption and sexual assault. In 2023, he was indicted four times, in particular for "conspiracy against the United States" at federal level, and for "false statements and documents, usurpation of public office, forgery and use of forgeries" in the state of Georgia.

Origins and youth

Family

Donald John Trump (/ˈdɑnəld d͡ʒɑn tɹʌmp/) was born on June 14, 1946 in the Jamaica neighborhood of Queens, New York. He is baptized and confirmed in his neighborhood Presbyterian church. The fourth of five children, he is the son of Fred Trump (1905-1999) and his wife Mary Anne Trump née MacLeod (1912-2000).

He has two brothers and two sisters: Maryanne (b. 1937), Fred Jr. (1938-1981), Elizabeth (b. 1942) and Robert (1948-2020). His elder brother, Fred Trump Jr. died of alcoholism, which prompted Donald Trump to take on the role of heir and abstain from alcohol and cigarettes.

Donald Trump's paternal family is of German origin, while his maternal family is from Scotland. His paternal grandparents came from Kallstadt. Donald Trump's grandfather, Frederick Trump, made his fortune running restaurants and boarding houses in the mushroom towns of Seattle and the Klondike. Donald's father Fred Trump, born in the Bronx, made a career as a real estate developer on the East Coast, while Mary Anne Trump was born in Tong, on the Scottish Isle of Lewis. Donald Trump is also the nephew of scientist John George Trump, who played a major role in the development of radiotherapy.

School

Donald Trump grew up in a Tudor Revival house in the chic Jamaica Estates neighborhood. He attended Kew-Forest School. At the age of thirteen - by his own admission a difficult teenager - he was sent by his parents, hoping to channel his energy, to the New York Military Academy (NYMA).

He then attended Fordham University in the Bronx for two years, starting in August 1964. He then enrolled at the Wharton School of the University of Pennsylvania, one of the few American institutions at the time to offer a specialized real estate curriculum. During his studies, he worked for the family business, Elizabeth Trump & Son (see *The Trump Organization*), named after his paternal grandmother. In May 1968, he graduated with a bachelor's degree in economics.

Trump was not drafted during the Vietnam War. During his studies, from 1964 to 1968, he was deferred four times. Then, after being deemed fit for service in 1966, he was discharged in October 1968. In a 2015 interview, he claims to have been discharged because of a heel spur. In 1969, he obtained a high number in the lottery organized for conscription in the United States, which would have enabled him to escape service in any case.

Business career

Debuts

During his studies, Donald Trump worked for his father's company, Elizabeth Trump and Son, which specialized in renting housing for middle-class New Yorkers in the boroughs of Brooklyn, Queens and Staten Island. While still a student, he worked with his father to reopen an apartment complex in Cincinnati.

In the early 1970s, he became president of the family business, while his father took over as chairman of the board. He then renamed the company The Trump Organization. In 1973, the Trump family was investigated by the Department of Justice for alleged discrimination against black prospective tenants. The Trump company finally signs an agreement to house tenants presented by the National Urban League.

One of their lawyers was Roy Cohn, who became an advisor and mentor to Donald Trump. In an interview with *Newsweek* in 1979, Trump said of him, "If you need someone who can get vicious against your opponents, you call on Roy".

Business expansion

In the 1970s, Donald Trump embarked on a career as an independent real estate developer, initially focusing on the Manhattan market. During his presidential campaign, he explains that he began with "a small loan of a million dollars" from his father, which he then repaid with interest.

In 1978, he made his first major deal when he bought a stake in the Commodore Hotel in New York. The hotel, then in a state of disrepair, underwent a costly renovation, largely financed by a $70 million loan negotiated by Fred Trump with the Hyatt Group. The hotel reopened as the Grand Hyatt Hotel.

In 1978, he completed negotiations to build Trump Tower, a 58-storey (202-metre) skyscraper in Midtown. The building, completed in 1983, houses the penthouse that serves as Donald Trump's principal residence, as well as the headquarters of the Trump Organization and a television studio. Trump Tower later served as the set for the TV show *The Apprentice*.

In 1986, Trump renovated the Wollman Rink, Central Park's famous open-air skating rink, which had suffered disastrous delays, costing $13 million over six years. Trump took over and completed the work in three months, saving $750,000 on a budget of $3 million. He earns the right to attach his name to the site's activities. In 2003, The Trump Organization was awarded the concession for a seasonal amusement park, Victorian Gardens (en).

In 1988, Trump purchased the Plaza Hotel for $400 million, entrusting its management and renovation to his wife at the time, Ivana. Although substantial, the hotel's income proved insufficient to offset the debts arising from the cost of the work. In 1995, Trump sold it for $325 million to Saudi prince Al-Walid ben Talal Al Saoud.

Over the years, Donald Trump has built or bought numerous other buildings - apartment and office blocks, luxury hotels and more - including outside New York (Trump World Tower, Trump Building, Trump International Hotel and Tower, Old Post Office Pavilion, etc.).

In 1985, he purchased the luxury Mar-a-Lago residence in Palm Beach, Florida, for $5 million, plus an additional $3 million for furnishings. This became both his winter residence and a private club with an annual membership of $150,000. At the same time, in association with Chrysler CEO Lee Iacocca, he bought an apartment building in Palm Beach, which he renamed *Trump Plaza of the Palm Beaches*.

He gradually expanded his real estate activities outside the United States and invested, with varying degrees of success, in numerous countries including Canada, Israel,

India, Turkey, the United Arab Emirates, Panama, Qatar, South Korea, Uruguay, the United Kingdom, Ireland, the Philippines, etc.

Casinos in Atlantic City

In the 1980s, Donald Trump invested in the casino business in Atlantic City, New Jersey. The Holiday Corp group finances the construction by the Trump group of the *Trump Plaza* hotel-casino, opened in 1984. Trump manages the gaming business. Within the first year, the hotel's poor results led to serious tensions between Trump and Holiday Corp. Trump also acquired a building in Atlantic City for $320 million, the construction of which had been started by the Hilton Group. Construction was completed in 1985, and the hotel-casino-marina, run by Donald Trump's wife Ivana, opened under the name Trump's Castle (later renamed *Trump Marina Hotel Casino*)>.

In 1988, still in Atlantic City, Trump bought the *Taj Mahal* casino, then under construction. The establishment, renamed *Trump Taj Mahal,* reopened in April 1990 after a billion-dollar construction project, making it the most expensive casino ever built. Financed to the tune of $675 million by *junk bonds* with an interest rate of 14%, the establishment filed for bankruptcy the following year. Both Trump Plaza and Trump's Castle fell victim to competition from the Trump Taj Mahal, and in 1991 had to negotiate a financial restructuring with their creditors.

The Taj Mahal turned around its fortunes in October 1991 when Trump sold 50% of his shares to his creditors, in exchange for a reduction in interest rates and a delay in paying off his debts. He was also forced to sell his *Trump Shuttle* airline and his *Trump Princess* yacht. The establishment was bought back in 1996 and reorganized under the banner of *Trump Hotels & Casino Resorts* (later renamed Trump Entertainment Resorts), a subsidiary which Trump chaired from mid-1995 to early 2009, and of which he was CEO from 2000 to 2005. Trump Entertainment Resorts filed for bankruptcy in 2004 with 1.8 billion in debt, then again in 2009 with 500 million in debt. A new restructuring plan enables Donald Trump to retain a 10% stake in the Trump Taj Mahal and its other casinos: in exchange, he continues to grant the establishments use of the Trump brand.

The Trump Marina Hotel Casino was sold to the Landry's group in 2011. A victim of the crisis in Atlantic City's casino sector, the Trump Plaza closes its doors in September 2014. After years of loss-making operations, the Trump Taj Mahal is sold in February 2016 to Carl Icahn, who must close it in October of the same year.

Golf courses

The Trump Organization manages several golf courses, in the United States and around the world; *Golfweek* magazine counted eighteen courses owned or managed by the group in 2015. For 2015, Trump declared to the Federal Election Commission a personal income of around $382 million linked to his golf activities. Donald Trump, himself an avid golfer, has stated that these investments represent the part of his business to which he is most attached.

In 2006, Trump acquired 570 hectares at Balmedie in Aberdeenshire, Scotland. He built a golf course there, despite the opposition of some local residents, on an area that had been declared a Site of Special Scientific Interest. In 2011, this story was the subject of the documentary *You've Been Trumped,* which explored the conflict between Trump and the residents. At the time, the businessman promised to create 6,000 local jobs with his land, but in 2016, he admitted to having generated only 200. In June 2015, he took legal action to prevent the construction of a wind farm near his golf course, but was ultimately unsuccessful by the UK Supreme Court.

In 2012, he acquired the *Doral Golf Resort & Spa* in Miami, which he renovated and renamed *Trump National Doral*; the course hosts the WGC-Cadillac Championship, an annual tournament of the World Golf Championships. In 2015, he declared it one of his most profitable ventures: sales at Trump National Doral in 2014 were estimated at $49.4 million.

In April 2014, Trump acquired the Trump Turnberry sports complex in Ayrshire, Scotland, which regularly hosts the men's British Open. After a major renovation project, the complex reopened in June 2016.

Other investments

Sports

In September 1983, Trump acquired the New Jersey Generals, an American soccer team in the United States Football League (USFL). Trump tried to compete directly with the National Football League and force a merger between the two leagues to increase the value of his investments. After the 1985 season, his team merged with the Houston Gamblers, but experienced major financial problems. The USFL finally ceased operations in 1986.

Despite his failure in American soccer, Trump continued to invest in sports, particularly golf. He also hosted several boxing matches at Atlantic City's Trump Plaza, including Michael Spinks' 1988 fight against Mike Tyson, for whom he was financial advisor for a time.

In 1989 and 1990, Trump gave his name to the Tour de Trump, a cycling race he wanted to equal the Tour de France and the Tour of Italy. He gave up after the second edition, due to the financial difficulties of his main companies at the time. The race continued for several years under the name Tour DuPont.

In 2014, he tried unsuccessfully to buy the Buffalo Bills team after the death of their previous owner, Ralph Wilson.

Beauty contest

From 1996 to 2015, Trump owned the Miss Universe, Miss USA and Miss Teen USA beauty pageants. Dissatisfied with the conditions under which his pageants were broadcast on CBS, he transferred them to NBC in 2002.

In 2015, at the start of Trump's presidential campaign, NBC and Univision ended their relationship with the Miss Universe pageant, due to the candidate's polemical remarks about Mexican illegal immigrants. Trump sued Univision, claiming $500 million for breach of contract and defamation. On September 11 of the same year, Trump announced that he was now the sole owner of Miss Universe, having purchased the shares from NBC, with whom the dispute had been settled out of court. Shortly afterwards, he sold his shares to William Morris/IMG. The dispute with Univision was also settled out of court in February 2016.

Model agency

In 1999, Donald Trump founded *Trump Model Management, a modeling* agency based in Manhattan's SoHo district. In conjunction with another company in his group, Trump Management Group LLC, after 2000 the agency brought in almost 250 foreign models for employment in the American fashion industry. In the course of 2016, Trump Model Management ran into serious difficulties, with several models and staff leaving during Donald Trump's presidential campaign. The Trump Organization eventually closed the subsidiary in April 2017.

Air transport

In 1989, Trump launched the *Trump Shuttle* airline, offering customers a luxury service. However, the company failed to turn a profit. By 1992, he was forced to sell the subsidiary, partly due to the financial difficulties of the Trump Taj Mahal casino. In 2008, the Trump Organization joined forces with Sentient Flight Group to offer a private jet service.

Trump University

In 2005, Donald Trump and his partners Michael Sexton and Jonathan Spitalny founded *Trump University LLC, a* professional training institute offering real estate courses priced between $1,500 and $35,000. After being ordered by the State of New York to stop using the name "university", the company was renamed *Trump Entrepreneurial Institute* in 2010. Trump is also personally implicated for failing to apply for the license required to open a school.

In 2013, the State of New York launched a lawsuit claiming $40 million from *Trump Entrepreneurial Institute* for false advertising. At the same time, two class action lawsuits are launched against *Trump Entrepreneurial Institute* by former students who feel they have been cheated. During his presidential campaign, Trump protested several times against the magistrate in charge of the cases, Judge Gonzalo P. Curiel, whom he accused of bias because of his Mexican origins. He later backtracked on his statements, explaining that his doubts about Curiel's impartiality were due not to the latter's origins, but to his handling of the case.

The Trump Entrepreneurial Institute trial, scheduled to take place in San Diego on November 28, 2016, has finally been cancelled, the parties having reached an out-of-court settlement in all three cases shortly after Trump's victory in the presidential election. Although denying having committed any crime, Trump agrees, in order to escape a trial that would have taken place before his inauguration as President of the United States, to pay $25 million to the 6,000 plaintiffs and to pay $1 million in fines for violating education laws. The agreement was reached just one hour before a court hearing scheduled to rule on a request by Trump to postpone the trial.

Marketing the Trump name and brand

One of Donald Trump's best-known traits as a businessman is his tendency to christen or rename most of the places, companies and products associated with him, and to market the most diverse goods and services under that label. The Trump brand - which includes Trump perfume, Trump tea, Trump vodka, Trump ties, Trump mattresses and even Trump Steaks - earned him $9.5 million in royalties for the period from early 2014 to mid-2015. In 2011, *Forbes* financial experts estimated the value of the Trump brand at $200 million. Trump disputed this analysis and claimed it was worth thirteen billion.

Bankruptcies

Donald Trump has never declared personal bankruptcy, but six of his hotels and casinos went bankrupt between 1991 and 2009. These were Trump Taj Mahal in 1991 (see *Hard Rock Hotel & Casino Atlantic City*), Trump Plaza Hotel and Casino in 1992, Plaza Hotel in 1992, Trump Castle Hotel and Casino in 1992, Trump Hotels and Casino Resorts in 2004 and Trump Entertainment Resorts in 2009. Donald Trump's companies used the provisions of Chapter 11 of the U.S. Bankruptcy Code, which allowed them to continue operating during the negotiations. Trump claimed in 2011 to have taken advantage of the legal possibilities of bankruptcy, in order to reduce his debts.

In the run-up to the 2016 presidential election, *The Economist* magazine, analyzing Donald Trump's career as a businessman, judges that his results have been mediocre overall compared with the rest of the New York real estate sector and stock market. The newspaper points out that information on Trump's financial empire is incomplete, due to his opaque and highly personal management style. It also questions Trump's ability to manage an organization larger than his own group. *The Washington Post* describes Donald Trump's career as a mixture of rodomontades, failures and genuine successes, and points out that, while he has a real gift when it comes to real estate, his experiences in other sectors have been less convincing. The newspaper concludes that the businessman's "genius" consisted first and foremost in creating a mythology around himself and his name.

Personal wealth and taxes

In 1982, the Forbes list of the richest Americans estimated Donald Trump's personal wealth at around $200 million, including his share of his father's inheritance. He was absent from this list between 1990 and 1995 due to major financial losses.

On June 26, 2015, when announcing his candidacy, Trump published a document estimating his fortune at $8,737,540,000, commenting on the occasion that he was "really rich". *Forbes questioned* these figures, estimating his real fortune at 4.1 billion.

In 2015, Trump's controversial statements on illegal immigrants caused him to lose, according to *Forbes*, around $125 million worth of contracts with companies such as NBCUniversal, Univision Network, or Macy's. His presidential campaign has also had a negative impact on his wealth, with some consumers boycotting his companies' products and services to mark their opposition to his candidacy. Attendance at Trump-owned hotels and casinos fell sharply in 2016.

In November 2016, *Forbes* estimated his personal wealth at $3.7 billion and ranked him 324 richest in the world and 113 richest in the US.

Trump has repeatedly refused to release his full tax returns, including during his 2016 presidential campaign. He is the first US presidential candidate to refuse to do so in 45 years.

In October 2016, the American media revealed that Donald Trump had declared a loss of $916 million to the IRS in 1995. Caused by the bankruptcies of three of his casinos and his airline, as well as by the risky purchase of the Plaza Hotel in Manhattan, these accumulated financial losses allowed him a tax deduction, spread over a period of eighteen years on his taxable income. He was thus able to significantly reduce, or even cancel, the sums he owed to the tax authorities. Trump acknowledged the veracity of this information, but refused to say which years were involved. Asked during a presidential debate about the tax deduction he had taken, he replied that the fact that he had used this provision proved his intelligence.

In March 2017, MSNBC published the two main pages of the Trump couple's tax return for 2005. These show that he paid $38 million in federal income tax that year, an effective rate of over 25%, due to the application of the "*alternative minimum tax*", designed to prevent taxpayers from taking advantage of tax loopholes to pay little or no tax, and which Donald Trump wants to have abolished. However, this information only partially answers the questions raised in the media during the presidential campaign, concerning the opacity maintained by Trump on his tax situation for 18 consecutive years.

On October 2, 2018, the *New York Times* published an investigation alleging that, far from the self-made man he claims to be, Donald Trump derived the beginnings of his personal fortune from tax evasion schemes initiated by his father. According to the daily, Donald Trump and his siblings benefited from payments made through a shell company set up by Fred Trump to conceal gifts to his children from the tax authorities. The investigation concludes that the sums paid to Donald Trump by his father, far from being limited to a million-dollar loan to launch a solo business, amounted to $413 million, part of which was received as part of a tax evasion scheme. The New York State Internal Revenue Service announced the opening of an investigation. The facts, if established, are not criminal due to the statute of limitations, but could result in a civil fine.

In 2022, he was fined $10,000 a day for failing to submit documents to the tax authorities relating to an investigation into the Trump Organization group that began in 2019. He eventually paid the $110,000 fine on May 19, 2022.

Media coverage and careers

As a businessman, Donald Trump is characterized by a constant quest for publicity: his communication strategy is also characterized by a pronounced taste for hyperbole, which leads him to announce each of his projects with an abundance of superlatives. Since the 1980s, he has been the subject of intense media attention in the United States, making him a familiar figure to the American public. The media began to take an interest in him in the first half of the decade: in May 1984, he appeared on the cover of *GQ* magazine. In November 1987, he published *Trump: The Art of the Deal*, a book co-authored with journalist Tony Schwarz (en), but of which he reportedly did not write a single line. The book, a mix of autobiography and business advice, was a huge bestseller and spent thirteen weeks at the top of the New York Times bestseller list. It was with this book, in which he extols his qualities as a businessman and presents himself as a model of American success, that Donald Trump became a national celebrity in the United States.

Subsequently, his fame earned him appearances in twelve feature films and fourteen TV series, usually in his own role. He appeared in such films as *Maman, j'ai encore raté l'avion!* (1992), Woody Allen's *Celebrity* (1998) and *Zoolander* (2001), as well as in episodes of The *Fresh Prince* (1996), *Sex and the City* (1999) and others. He also played a secondary role in the film *Les Chenapans* (1994), in which he played an oil tycoon. His roles earned him membership of the Screen Actors Guild and an annual pension of over $110,000. Frequently imitated and parodied by American humorists and cartoonists, he also hosted his own radio show for a time, entitled *Trumped!*

He is also often compared to Charles Foster Kane, the main character in Orson Welles' masterpiece *Citizen Kane*, which he describes as his favorite film.

The Apprentice

In 2004, Trump became the executive producer and host of the NBC reality show *The Apprentice*, in which candidates compete for a senior management position in one of the Trump Group's companies. Candidates are eliminated from the game by Donald Trump himself, whose catchphrase on the show is "You're fired! The first year of *The Apprentice* paid Trump $50,000 per episode (around $700,000 for the whole season), but the success of the show meant he was paid $1 million per episode thereafter. The show also spawned a *spin-off, The Celebrity Apprentice*. In 2007, the show earned Trump a star on the Hollywood Walk of Fame for his contribution to television entertainment. Trump hosted fourteen seasons of *The Apprentice*, from January 2004 to February 2015. In 2016, his Hollywood Walk of Fame star was vandalized during his presidential campaign.

World Wrestling Entertainment

From the late 1980s onwards, Donald Trump fueled his media fame by associating himself with the world of wrestling. He rented the Trump Plaza in Atlantic City from the World Wrestling Federation (WWF) to host *WrestleMania IV* on March 27, 1988, then *WrestleMania V* on April 2, 1989. During both editions, the director uses close-ups of him in the front row. The Trump Taj Mahal in Atlantic City hosted the World Bodybuilding Federation Championship, which at the time belonged to World Wrestling Entertainment (then called the *World Wrestling Federation*).

Trump appears in person at various WWE events, most notably at WrestleMania 23 in 2007 for a match called *The Battle of the* Billionaires. During this event, he supported Bobby Lashley, while Vince McMahon backed Lashley's opponent, Umaga, with both businessmen promising to have their heads shaved if their champion lost the match. In the end, it was McMahon who complied, after Lashley's victory.

In 2009, Vince McMahon announced that he was selling *RAW* to Donald Trump, who then became the owner of the *WWE Raw* wrestling show, renaming it *TRUMP RAW*. However, the following week, McMahon buys back *Monday Night Raw* for double the sold price. In 2013, Trump became a member of the WWE Hall of Fame in recognition of his role in promoting World Wrestling Entertainment. In 2016, Linda McMahon, wife of Vince McMahon and longtime WWE director, donates $6 million to Donald Trump for his presidential campaign. She was appointed head of the *Small Business Administration* (SBA) after his victory.

Political ascent

First commitments

Initially affiliated with the Democratic Party, Donald Trump later became a fervent supporter of President Ronald Reagan. He then joined the Republican Party.

In September 1987, shortly before the release of his autobiography, he bought a full-page ad in several major newspapers to publish an "open letter" addressed "to the American people", in which he advocated an isolationist policy to revive the U.S. economy. In the wake of his book's success, he considered running for president in 1988, forming a ticket with Oprah Winfrey as vice-presidential candidate. George H. W. Bush, who won the election, reportedly considered forming a ticket with Trump.

Subsequently, Trump has repeatedly considered running for office, but has so far failed to follow through on his candidacy plans.

Affiliation with the Reform Party

He left the Republican Party in 1999 to join the Reform Party of the United States of America, founded by Ross Perot. He sought the party's nomination for the 2000 presidential election, but withdrew his candidacy despite receiving 7% of the national vote should he win the party's nomination.

Presidency of George W. Bush

Between 2001 and 2009, under President George W. Bush, he was again registered as a Democratic voter.

He was critical of the Iraq war in March 2003, but also spoke of the economic interests that the United States could derive from the conflict. Judging that Saddam Hussein had at least the merit of "killing terrorists", he publicly disavowed the Iraq war from 2004 onwards. During the 2016 presidential campaign, despite George W. Bush's popularity among Republican voters, Donald Trump opposed the neoconservatives and described the 2003 intervention as a "foreign policy disaster", portraying the Bush presidency more generally as a failure. In the run-up to the 2016 presidential election, George H. W. Bush declares that he will vote for Hillary Clinton, while George W. Bush declares that he will vote white.

In 2005, Donald Trump defined himself as a "mix" of Democrat and Republican. In 2008, he helped finance Hillary Clinton's campaign for the Democratic nomination. During the presidential campaign, he declared that George W. Bush should have been removed from office because of the war in Iraq, but, a staunch supporter of the Republican Party, backed John McCain, whom he said would "make a great president".

Barack Obama's presidency

In 2009, he joined the Republican Party, and rejoined in 2012 after several years without political affiliation. In 2015, Donald Trump declared that he "[recognized] himself as a Democrat in certain respects" and explained his earlier Democratic tropism by the influence of living in Manhattan, reputed to be a historically Democratic land.

After considering a bid as an independent in the 2012 presidential election, he threw his support behind Republican candidate Mitt Romney. After Barack Obama's re-election, he calls to "march on Washington and stop this charade". Journalists speculate that Trump considered running for president after the 2011 White House Correspondents' Dinner, during which Barack Obama repeatedly mocked Donald Trump.

In 2011, Donald Trump took up the theory that Barack Obama was not born in the United States, but in Kenya, which would make him ineligible to become President of the United States. He also claims that Obama's grades were insufficient for him to enter Harvard Law School. Academic Gregory Benedetti believes that stoking this controversy then allowed Trump to become "the standard-bearer for an ultra-conservative branch eager to present Obama as an outsider, a cultural and identity Other". Trump supported this conspiracy theory for five years, notably through numerous tweets. In September 2016, he declared that Obama had indeed been born in the United States.

He also opposes several measures taken by President Obama, notably the *Patient Protection and Affordable Care Act*, as well as his migration policy.

Presidential election 2016

Republican primaries

Trump announced his candidacy for the Republican primaries on June 16, 2015, with the slogan "*Make America Great Again*" - once used by Ronald Reagan, presenting himself as the savior of a moribund America, undermined by the corruption of its elites and an iniquitous electoral system.

A few days after announcing his candidacy, when he was polling at less than 5%, he made an unexpected breakthrough in the polls, even though Jeb Bush was still considered the favorite. From July onwards, polls put him at the top of primary voting intentions, with support estimated at between 17% and 40% nationwide. During the summer of 2015, he topped the list of personalities searched on Google and cited on social networks. This unexpected "Trump effect" gave media coverage to the primaries: the first debate between the Republican candidates, on August 6, 2015, focused on him and attracted 24 million viewers, eight times more than in 2011. Doubts about the durability of his candidacy, often scorned, disappeared at the end of summer 2015.

However, most commentators continued to predict his defeat. As soon as he declared his candidacy, he set himself apart by using Twitter in a highly polemical way, in particular to attack, even insult, anyone who displeased him. He appointed a communications director for social networks, Dan Scavino. In October 2017, the *Washington Post* counted 385 people, groups, places, organizations, institutions, etc., insulted by Trump on Twitter, sometimes repeatedly.

Right from the start of his campaign, he claimed to be "politically incorrect", particularly on the subject of immigration. He stirred up controversy by accusing Mexican immigrants of being "criminals" and "rapists", whom the Mexican government would "actively" send to the United States, and by proposing the construction of a wall along the Mexican border - his platform's flagship measure. He provoked another outcry by advocating "a total and complete halt to the entry of Muslims into the United States", and was generally criticized for statements deemed sexist or racist. Trump's campaign quickly attracted the attention of the international media, due to his atypical personality and outspoken statements: he wrote on Twitter that global warming was an invention of the Chinese to undermine the American economy, suggested that journalist Megyn Kelly had been aggressive with him because she was menstruating, and publicly mocked the disability of another journalist whose questions had displeased him.

In February 2016, after a disappointing showing in the Iowa caucus (24.3% of the vote), he came out well ahead in New Hampshire (35.2%), South Carolina (32.5%) and Nevada (45.8%), reinforcing his favorite status. On *Super Tuesday,* March 1, 2016, he consolidated his lead by winning seven of the eleven states at stake. While he was attacked by Mitt Romney and John McCain in particular, political action committees launched a campaign against him, running negative ads costing tens of millions of dollars. Marco Rubio, one of his main opponents, withdrew from the race on March 15.

He then received the support of various Republican figures. After Sarah Palin in January, Chris Christie rallied behind Trump, followed by Jeff Sessions - the first Republican congressman to do so - his former rival Ben Carson, then Rudy Giuliani.

In the recent history of the U.S. presidential primaries, Trump is one of the poll favorites to have spent the least money. As of March 10, 2016, he has spent the smallest campaign budget of any Republican or Democratic candidate, at $27 million (Marco Rubio $85 million, Bernie Sanders $96 million, Ted Cruz $104 million and Hillary Clinton $188 million). He spends a lot on mailings to voters and merchandising, but does not commission any polls (whereas Hillary Clinton spent $896,000 on polls in April alone), and spends very little on advertising or grassroots campaigning, relying instead on big rallies and lots of media airtime thanks to his polemical statements - he is probably the most closely followed candidate in the history of American political campaigns.

On April 19, he won the state of New York with almost 60% of the vote, becoming the only candidate able to collect the 1,237 delegates needed to secure the nomination on the first ballot at the Republican Party convention in July. His two remaining rivals, Ted Cruz and John Kasich, then reached an agreement whereby one of them would withdraw from certain primaries in May and June, to avoid a dispersal of votes and block Trump. However, his landslide victory (53%) in the Indiana primary on May 3 led Cruz and Kasich to suspend their campaigns, thereby securing Trump the nomination.

Reince Priebus, chairman of the Republican National Committee, then called on the party to unite behind him. Almost all the other participants in the Republican primary rallied behind Trump. However, some 50 major Republican Party donors decided not to support him. Former President George H. W. Bush and his sons, former President George W. Bush and former Florida Governor Jeb Bush, also announced that they would not support him.

On May 25, he surpassed the number of delegates required to win the nomination. With a duel against Hillary Clinton on the horizon, a series of polls showed him winning or tied. After enlisting the services of *spin doctor* Paul Manafort in March, he thanked his campaign manager, Corey Lewandowski, in June, reflecting the "professionalization" of his campaign, according to Reince Priebus.

The success of his candidacy contradicts the tactics envisaged by Republican Party strategists, for whom the successive defeats of John McCain and Mitt Romney should have led to greater moderation in order not to alienate the fast-growing Hispanic electorate. Soufian Alsabbagh, a specialist in the American right, believes that Donald Trump embodies the culmination of a "radicalization movement" in the Republican Party following the successive candidacies of George W. Bush, John McCain and Mitt Romney. According to political scientist Alix Meyer, "you have to go back to Barry Goldwater, in 1964, to find such a disconnect between the nominated candidate and the party apparatus of which he claims to be a part"; his colleague Marc Landy evokes the profiles of William Jennings Bryan in 1896 and George McGovern in 1972. We have to go back to the candidacy of Dwight D. Eisenhower in 1952 to see a political novice win the Republican nomination. Political scientist Marc Landy points out that Donald Trump practices "an entertainment populism, in the manner of Silvio Berlusconi, which is not in American habits", through "a level of incivility usual in many media, but uncommon in the political arena", frequently insulting his opponents, giving them nicknames (Ted "the liar", Bush "the soft" or "little" Marco) or fueling rumors about them, such as Ted Cruz's father's involvement in the assassination of President Kennedy. In August 2016, he was accused of implicitly calling for Hillary Clinton's murder during a rally. In addition, clashes between his supporters and opponents regularly punctuate his rallies. On June 18, 2016, while at a rally in Las Vegas, he escaped an assassination attempt by a 20-year-old British man who had tried to seize a duty officer's gun.

Presidential campaign

On July 16, 2016, Donald Trump announced that Indiana Governor Mike Pence, initially a Ted Cruz supporter, would be his presidential running mate. The "ticket" was officially invested by the Republican Party on July 19, 2016, at the Cleveland convention. Donald Trump congratulated himself on obtaining "the largest number of votes ever obtained in the history of the Republican Party" (over 14 million). Unexpectedly, Ted Cruz, who had come second in the primary, refused to endorse the Republican candidate and called on American voters to vote "according to their conscience" during his speech in

Cleveland. In his nomination speech, he paints a bleak picture of the United States, using a rhetoric that is both nationalist and populist. The first night of the convention was a great success in terms of audience ratings for the television stations that broadcast it, with CNN in particular enjoying a 200% increase over the 2012 event.

Shortly after his inauguration, polls continue to show Trump neck-and-neck with the Democratic candidate, while both suffer from a poor public image. Opinion polls for August are unfavorable to Trump, who is trailing by between 6 and 8 points. At the same time, Paul Manafort resigned from his campaign team because of his involvement in a corruption case in Ukraine. Trump then created the post of "campaign general manager", which he entrusted to an atypical and controversial figure, Steve Bannon, head of the far-right website *Breitbart News*. At the same time, he promoted Kellyanne Conway, whose profile is consensual within the Republican establishment, to campaign manager. Shortly afterwards, he expressed "regret" for his remarks, which "may have hurt people personally", and inflected one of his proposals against illegal immigration for the first time. On August 31, 2016, at the end of a visit to Mexico where he spoke alongside President Enrique Peña Nieto, he reaffirmed his hard line on immigration. At the same time, he is trying to broaden his audience in the African-American community, traditionally very supportive of the Democrats. Polls in

September 2016 saw voting intentions in his favor approaching those for Hillary Clinton.

Initially lagging far behind Hillary Clinton, the pace of his fundraising picked up sharply in the summer of 2016, thanks to a massive number of small donations of a few dozen dollars made online, and thus tended to close the gap. While American banks refuse to lend him money because of his poor relations with them as an entrepreneur, his biggest donors are Russian oligarchs close to the Kremlin. The main pro-Republican backers refrain from funding him, preferring to support candidates in the forthcoming legislative elections. While Donald Trump enjoys the support of the majority of Marco Rubio's and especially Ted Cruz's donors, those of Jeb Bush, John Kasich and Chris Christie are funding Hillary Clinton's campaign to a greater extent.

Donald Trump's team aired its first general election ads in August 2016, while Hillary Clinton's team had already spent $61 million and the other two candidates, Jill Stein and Gary Johnson, had also produced spots. The bulk of his expenses were then devoted to travel and event-related costs, while his team remained extremely small. He prefers to secure free publicity on social networks and in the media, or to rely on the Republican Party's infrastructure for logistics and fundraising. As of mid-September 2016, Donald Trump has spent $18.7 million on TV spots, compared with Hillary Clinton's $109.4 million, and he has raised $205.8 million in funds, compared with Hillary Clinton's $516.7 million. He has the support of just 6 newspapers, compared with over 200 for Hillary Clinton, according to a count by *Politico,* which estimates that "no candidate has ever received so few endorsements" from the press.

Some observers have drawn comparisons with the 1996 election, given that Republican candidate Bob Dole fell behind in the polls early on, and that most of the party's congressional candidates in subsequent elections also considered the runoff a foregone conclusion.

On September 27, the first televised debate between the two candidates appeared to be won by Hillary Clinton. In the three weeks leading up to the election, Trump's campaign becomes more radical and he suggests that the election is rigged, in particular because of the media's bias against him. This attitude drew criticism from Barack Obama.

Political communication

Trump was able to use several communication strategies to his advantage during the election, thanks to a particular mobilization within the American population. Through an emotional demonstration to the American demographic that is riddled with cultural marginalization and deep sensitivity, Donald Trump leaves behind traditional norms of socialization and reaches out primarily to white working-class communities. He does this by creating an identity similar to that of the common citizen and speaking openly about his views in relation to racial and ethnic differences, while justifying how this affects the economy. Trump focused on working-class Americans who had to work hard, while bureaucrats and government administrators profited behind their backs. With the slogan of "Make America Great Again", Donald Trump was able to rally a section of the American population around the idea that a decline in the economic and cultural status of Americans was taking place and that this status needed to be reclaimed.

Various concepts are important to mention when looking at the communication strategies employed by Trump to advance his election campaign. The power of the speaker is of paramount importance when we see how the charisma of a political leader can be instrumentalized in a communicative framework to advance a message, develop support for that message and transform it into mass mobilization. This charisma manifests itself in a grandiose, narcissistic self-promotion. Moreover, through his use of captivating political rhetoric, in some cases employing a more commanding tone and often with a dynamic expression, many would say that Donald Trump is an orator who knows how to rally his audience. Several icons and specific aspects of these strategies are evident from a communicative analysis, such as the stereotypes he uses with the aim of creating a ruckus among the population, his use of similarity, the strategic use of populism that is apparent when he appeals to the white middle-class American citizen, and his use of strategic terms like "them" and "us" to mobilize his adherents. Trump has been able to use political communication to his advantage thanks to the emphasis placed on the identity roles, emotions and powerful narratives of the 45 President of the United States.

Certain effects and lessons on the use of political communication around the world need to be mentioned when analyzing Donald Trump's communication. Firstly, Trump has demonstrated the importance and power of political communication. Through communicative vectors, such as on media networks in the eyes of huge numbers of people, directly to a large audience, or any other form of contemporary media that reaches huge numbers of people, Trump has been able to rally the American people around his message. Secondly, the way Trump expressed himself in this election doesn't qualify as traditionally presidential.

Thus, political marketing and the pressure of group campaigns and social movements characterize the political rhetoric that has been able to influence the people. Trump has been able to instrumentalize his political strategies through the media and create an electoral campaign that transcends time, as it opens the door to a new way of conceiving and practicing politics and winning elections. Thirdly, Donald J. Trump is the first president characterized as a political figure who has been able to use the more humorous side of politics to his advantage to attract more people to him and create a unique relationship with the American people. The power of humor in persuasion and rhetoric is important, and Trump's ability to create a form of entertainment politics is unique in the history of political communication.

In recent times, the use of extremist, violent or controversial rhetoric to incite individuals already inclined towards aggression has encouraged the development of a more inflammatory relationship with a political leader. Trump has thus revolutionized the language, symbols and mediatization that will be used across political communication in the future to mobilize a people around an ideological advance. Finally, the militarization of political communication is a powerful and dangerous tool when analyzing mass persuasion and propaganda.

Accusations of sexism and sexual assault

A few days before the second debate between Donald Trump and Hillary Clinton, the *Washington Post* released a video from 2005, in which Trump - recorded without his knowledge in the studio of the TV show *Des jours et des vies* - boasts of his womanizing and asserts to his interviewer that "When you're a star, [women] let you do whatever you want, grab them *by* the pussy, do whatever you want". The publication of this video provoked outraged reactions from within the ranks of the Republican Party, including that of his running mate Mike Pence, and the candidate apologized for his remarks, which he described as "locker-room bragging".

In the days that followed, several women publicly accused Donald Trump of having made unwelcome advances towards them, and even of having behaved in a manner tantamount to sexual assault, for example by forcing himself on them or kissing them. The Republican candidate denies having behaved in this way and retaliates in his own way during the second debate opposing Hillary Clinton, on October 9, 2016: he recalls that women have accused her husband, Bill Clinton, of having sexually assaulted or raped them, and brings four of them to attend the debate. In response, rapper Will.i.am released a satirical video on October 14 entitled Grab'm by the *Pussy, in* which he denounced Trump's contemptuous attitude and sexist comments towards women.

Untruths

Before embarking on his presidential campaign, Donald Trump had already developed the concept of "veridical hyperbole" back in the 1980s, explaining in one of his books, "People want to believe in the greatest, the most awesome, the most spectacular. I call it truthful hyperbole. It's an innocent form of exaggeration - and a very effective method of promotion.

During the Republican primary campaign, he said of the September 11, 2001 attacks: "I saw, in New Jersey City, thousands and thousands of Muslim people cheering the fall of the World Trade Center towers", but there is no proof of these events, which the New Jersey authorities have denied. Very active on Twitter during the presidential campaign, he claims "Whites killed by whites: 16%. Whites killed by blacks: 81%", with a graphic to back it up. He relies on a source (the "San Francisco Bureau of Crime Statistics") that doesn't exist, and actually inverts the figures, since 82.4% of whites murdered were killed by whites and 14.8% by blacks. He claims that the "true unemployment rate in the U.S. is 42%", adding up the "inactive", mixing retirees, pre-retirees, stay-at-home moms, students and high-schoolers to arrive at this erroneous count. Donald Trump also explains that "American growth has never been negative" and that the US GDP growth rate went into negative territory in the first quarter of 2015 under Barack Obama's presidency, adding "this has never happened in history". However, the first claim is false, and as for the second, the American media note that this has happened 42 times since the Second World War. During the campaign, he constantly asserted that the elections were "rigged", developing several "conspiracy theories" on the subject. After his victory thanks to his majority in the Electoral College, but with over two million votes less than Hillary Clinton in the popular vote, he wrote on Twitter: "In addition to winning the Electoral College, I won the popular vote if you deduct the millions of people who voted illegally", without putting forward the slightest proof. The Politifact website finds 76% complete or partial lies in Donald Trump's statements for 2015, putting him at the top of the list of American political figures whose statements are most often "arch-false, false or rather false".

Media positioning

More than 76% of the American press supports Hillary Clinton, compared with less than 5% for Donald Trump. Many press titles traditionally calling for a vote for the Republican candidate are opposed to him. Despite the support of Rupert Murdoch's *New York Post* and *The National Enquirer* during the Republican primary, extremely negative articles are published daily about Donald Trump.

During the campaign, Rupert Murdoch's media group, notably the Fox News television network, actively supported Trump's candidacy. This was also the case for the far-right website Breitbart News, whose director Steve Bannon left to run the Republican candidate's final campaign, before becoming a White House strategic advisor.

Following Donald Trump's victory in the presidential election, influential media such as *The New York Times* admit that they failed to capture the anger of a section of the American electorate. Paul Krugman, winner of the Nobel Prize in Economics in 2008, highlights the ignorance of "elite" America for "deep" America, and Margaret Sullivan (en), editorial writer for The *Washington Post*, paraphrases the thesis of Peter Thiel (Silicon Valley investor and Donald Trump supporter) when he explains that "journalists always take Trump at face value, but without taking him seriously" while "his voters, on the other hand, take him seriously, but don't take him at face value" and that therefore, "for example, when he proposes to build a wall on the Mexican border, journalists demand details, want to know how he's going to do it", while his voters "understand that he doesn't really want to build a wall and simply hear that he's proposing a sounder, smarter migration policy".

Victory over Hillary Clinton

On November 8, 2016, Donald Trump won the presidential election. He reversed the predicted trend, particularly in Florida and North Carolina, which the polls had overwhelmingly anticipated as favoring Hillary Clinton, as well as in Michigan, Wisconsin and Pennsylvania, traditionally Democratic, and which pollsters had also predicted as leaning towards the Democratic camp. These five states gave him a total of 74 electoral votes. His protectionist, anti-illegal immigration stance enabled him to gain a strong foothold in the *Rust Belt*, a formerly industrial region that has suffered the full brunt of offshoring and free-trade policies. He was awarded a total of 306 electoral votes to his rival's 232. The latter obtained 2.87 million votes (2.1 percentage points) more than him. Such a situation, due to the indirect voting system and the practice of *winner takes all*, has occurred only four times in the past, in the presidential elections of 1824, 1876, 1888 and 2000. Such a discrepancy in terms of number of votes (but not percentage) is an all-time record for this electoral system, rekindling criticism of it and calls for its reform (Donald Trump opposed the system in 2012).

Donald Trump won among voters over 45 (53%, vs. 45% for Clinton), male voters (53%, vs. 41% for Clinton), low-education voters (51% of voters with no more than junior high or high school and 53% of voters with some college but no degree, vs. 45% and 43% for Clinton respectively), white voters (58%, vs. 37% for Clinton) and heterosexual voters (48%, vs. 47% for Clinton).

This victory belies the projections. Out of a sample of 376 polls published between May 2015 and November 2016, only 30 showed Donald Trump in the lead; the last ones published predicted a lead of around 3.5 percentage points for Hillary Clinton, and a clear victory for her in terms of the grand electors. Throughout his campaign, most political scientists had predicted that he would lose, and many commentators maintain that his victory is improbable, if not impossible. In the aftermath of the election, the American media, which supported Hillary Clinton by 75% and Donald Trump by less than 5%, confess to having been unable to capture the feeling of the deep country.

Green candidate Jill Stein files requests for a recount in three states where the results were close, but the operation confirms Trump's victory in Wisconsin, and is overturned by the federal courts in Michigan.

Donald Trump becomes the oldest and wealthiest president ever elected by Americans to a first term, ahead of George Washington, and the only one to reach this position without having previously held an elective office and/or military responsibilities. In his book *Fire and Fury: Trump in the White House*, published in January 2018, Michael Wolff asserts that Donald Trump didn't actually want to become president and was primarily seeking publicity for himself, running in an election he never imagined he could win.

Transition period

On November 8, 2016, as Donald Trump was awarded 306 of the 538 electoral college electors, nominating the president for the White House, the Republican Party was also on the verge of controlling the House of Representatives, the Senate and therefore the Supreme Court. For political scientist Vincent Michelot, "this is unprecedented since the 1930s. Even Reagan governed with a Democratic majority in the House of Representatives". This is the sixth time since 1900 that Republicans have taken control of Congress and the White House.

Protests against his victory

As his election was followed by demonstrations in major American cities to protest his victory, he adopted an open and appeased tone in his first statements, including against former opponents whom he had harshly attacked during his campaign, Hillary Clinton in particular, specifying that he had no intention of "harming the Clintons" because "that would divide the country very much". In line with his campaign, he continued to express himself on Twitter in a polemical tone: he reacted to the demonstrations by saying that they were "professional protesters incited by the media", but backtracked by praising the demonstrators' "passion" "for our great country". In several tweets, he mocks and contradicts the *New York Times on the* subject of campaign monitoring and the transition period.

International approaches

He meets Indian businessmen, as well as Argentine President Mauricio Macri and Japanese Prime Minister Shinzō Abe. Faced with Donald Trump's repeated commitment to withdraw from the Trans-Pacific Partnership agreement, Chinese President Xi Jinping invites Asia-Pacific leaders to support the competing regional free trade agreement his country has proposed to them. According to some media reports, Donald Trump's decision explains the decision of John Key, Prime Minister of New Zealand and "fervent supporter" of the Trans-Pacific Partnership agreement, not to seek re-election. Shortly afterwards, Donald Trump held talks with Tsai Ing-wen, President of Taiwan, a first since diplomatic relations between the two states broke down in 1979; this exchange prompted a "solemn protest" from the Chinese leadership, followed by the White House's reaffirmation of its support for the "One China" policy. On Twitter, Donald Trump then accuses China of devaluing its currency to better compete with American companies and "building a vast military complex in the South China Sea".

On November 13, 2016, he announced that he would give up his salary as president ($400,000 a year) and would only receive the symbolic dollar he was required to by law.

He ended the transition period with the lowest public approval rating for a U.S. president in the previous two decades. Vincent Michelot emphasizes the "exceptional nature" of the transition period, which was conducted with a great deal of publicity, contrary to usual practice, and led to a significant delay in appointments: "This is all the more worrying as the ministers appointed have in common that they have no experience of the public sector. And that some of its members are not only inexperienced, but also hostile to the very existence of the ministry they are to head".

Election by the electoral college

As the presidential election is indirect in the United States, Donald Trump's definitive election is only effective once the Electoral College has voted. Up until the Electoral College meeting on December 19, 2016, the identities of many Republican electors were revealed by anti-Trump groups, and several of them were subjected to harassment and death threats to change their vote. Donald Trump nonetheless won 304 electoral votes to Hillary Clinton's 227, with only two electoral votes against his Democratic rival's five.

Appointments

During the transition period, Donald Trump surrounds himself with a transition team and begins to appoint the members of his future government. Based on known appointments as of December 13, 2016, the American website Quartz calculated that the 17 members of the future Trump administration had $9.5 billion at their disposal, as much as the 109 million poorest Americans. The appointment of wealthy financiers and businessmen and women to key positions, as well as the presence of numerous lobbyists on the transition team, were denounced by Democratic Senator Elizabeth Warren, who challenged the president-elect in a letter dated November 15, accusing him of "already failing" in his promise not to be in the hands of elites by appointing "a slew of Wall Street bankers, industry insiders and lobbyists to [his] transition team". The senator points out that "72% of Americans, Democrats and Republicans alike, believe that 'the American economy is rigged to benefit the rich and powerful'", and calls on Trump not to include these people on his team. In an interview with CBS television on November 13, the billionaire had explained that it was difficult to find people to work with the government without them having ties to lobbies, believing that Washington was, "in its entirety", a "huge lobby".

Position statements

In the weeks following his election, he made sure to keep his campaign promises concerning the preservation of jobs in American manufacturing companies. On November 29, 2016, heating manufacturer Carrier, which had planned to relocate 1,400 jobs to Mexico, announced that it would preserve 1,000 jobs in the country following negotiations with Donald Trump. On the following December 28, cell phone operator Sprint Nextel announced that it would be bringing 5,000 jobs back to the United States, and thanked Donald Trump for his involvement in the project. On January 3, 2017, the Ford automotive group, threatened by the President-elect with substantial import taxes, reverses its decision to build a new plant in Mexico, preferring to use part of the $1.6 billion earmarked for the project to develop a site in Michigan, hard hit by deindustrialization.

On January 3, 2017, under pressure from Donald Trump, Republican lawmakers backed away from curtailing the powers of the Office of Parliamentary Ethics, an independent body charged with investigating ethical violations by elected officials.

After Barack Obama's decision to expel 35 Russian diplomats over accusations of Russian interference in the election campaign, Donald Trump is skeptical and praises Vladimir Putin's "intelligence" in deciding not to retaliate. Against the backdrop of fears of a new Cold War, some observers point to Barack Obama's desire to put the president-elect in a difficult position. Once elected, he will ask Russia to "reduce violence in Ukraine and return Crimea".

After his election, Donald Trump continues to express himself extensively on Twitter, including on diplomatic matters. On January 5, 2017, China's official Xinhua news agency deplored his "obsession with Twitter diplomacy". After contradicting the One China principle, which caused tensions with Xi Jinping's regime, he finally acknowledged it in an interview with the latter in February 2017, which also reassured Japan.

On January 11, 2017, nine days before Trump's inauguration, Mexican President Enrique Peña Nieto affirmed, like his predecessor Vicente Fox, that his country would not pay for the wall promised by Trump during his campaign and estimated to cost $25 billion. Nevertheless, he says he is ready for open negotiations with the new president, particularly on immigration issues.

Before and after his election, leaders of European institutions such as Donald Tusk (President of the European Council), Martin Schulz (President of the European Parliament) and Pierre Moscovici (European Commissioner) expressed their distrust of him. In January 2017, Donald Trump declared that the European Union was "an instrument at the service of Germany". He calls the Brexit "a success for the United Kingdom". He sees the migration crisis in Europe and Germany's stance on the issue as the reason for their departure.

Trump is also critical of NATO, which he accuses of failing to adapt to the terrorist threat. He also deplores the fact that only five countries are meeting NATO's target of devoting 2% of GDP to military spending.

President of the United States

Investiture

Many artists refuse to take part in the inauguration of the new head of state on January 19 and 20, 2017. Country singer Toby Keith agrees to perform, and *America's Got Talent* winner Jackie Evancho sings the national anthem after the swearing-in.

Donald Trump officially becomes the 45 President of the United States by taking the oath of office on Capitol Hill in Washington, D.C. on January 20, 2017 at 12:00 p.m. EST (that's 6:00 p.m. CET).

A controversy erupted over the size of the crowd present on the Mall in Washington, D.C. on the day of his inauguration, estimated by many media outlets to be much smaller than that which attended Barack Obama's inauguration eight years earlier (the figures put forward are 250,000 people in 2017 versus 1.8 million in 2009), which the new president's team totally refutes, with White House spokesman Sean Spicer declaring: "It was the largest crowd ever to attend an inauguration, period" and adviser Kellyanne Conway explaining that she promotes "alternative facts".

The day after his inauguration, he was confronted with large-scale, mainly feminist protests, the largest of which, the Women's March on Washington, D.C., brought together between 500,000 and one million people. Similar demonstrations took place in 400 other American cities and 70 countries, with organizers estimating that between two and three million people took part. The inaugurations of presidents such as Richard Nixon in 1973, Ronald Reagan in 1981 and George W. Bush in 2001 also gave rise to demonstrations, albeit not on the same scale; the largest previous demonstration in 1973, for example, drew just 60,000 participants.

Simultaneously, during his visit to CIA headquarters, Donald Trump declared that he was at war with journalists, whom he described as "the most dishonest human beings on earth".

Appointments, dismissals and resignations

Key positions aside, Donald Trump's administration stands out for its significant backlog of senior appointments. As of June 2017, only 123 of the 558 key positions had been filled, with various nominees also having been rejected by the Senate. After two months, you have to go back to George Bush Sr. to find a more significant delay in setting up an administration. Many federal agencies are now operating in slow motion, with temporary or non-existent leaders.

There are several reasons for this unprecedented delay, starting with the slow pace of appointments: as of July 2017, the White House had not put forward any candidates for 357 of the 575 top posts. According to the New York Times, at that date Donald Trump had announced only 38% of his choices, compared with 78% for Barack Obama at the same time. Observers attribute this slowness to Trump's failure to launch the nominations process early enough, due to a lack of preparation. Also blamed is his desire to downsize the state apparatus, and to favor certain agencies over others, such as the Agency for International Development and the Environmental Protection Agency. On the other hand, Senate Democrats' opposition to the Trump administration's nominees has been labeled "obstructionism" by the Republican camp, which blames them for the confirmation, after six months in office, of only 60 out of 165 nominees. Democratic senators justify this slowness by the time taken to examine potential conflicts of interest linked to the candidacies of businessmen nominated by Trump.

Between January and August 2017, Donald Trump's inner circle at the White House saw twelve departures, a total unprecedented over such a period. In addition to those of Michael T. Flynn and Andrew Puzder, other high-ranking aides resigned, including White House Chief of Staff Reince Priebus at the end of July. Also at the end of July, Communications Director Sean Spicer was replaced by Anthony Scaramucci, who was forced to resign ten days later. These repeated departures and dismissals are largely explained by the investigation into links between his campaign team and Russia, as well as by his failures in Congress and internal rivalries.

In his first year as president, Donald Trump is set to replace more than a third of his advisors, representing an unprecedented "turnover" in the US government. In March 2018, the Brookings Institution estimated that nearly 43% of the administration's most senior positions had been subject to resignations or forced departures since Donald Trump took office. In December of the same year - marked by the resignations or dismissals of Secretary of State Rex Tillerson, National Economic Council Chairman Gary Cohn, National Security Adviser H. R. McMaster, EPA Administrator Scott Pruitt, Attorney General Jeff Sessions, U.N. Ambassador Nikki Haley, Secretary of the Interior Ryan Zinke, Chief of Staff John F. Kelly and Secretary of Defense James Mattis - the Trump administration reached a 62% rate of departures among its top officials, compared to 24% under Barack Obama,

33% under George W. Bush and 38% under Bill Clinton at the same stage of their respective terms.

Domestic policy

Economy and society

As soon as he was nominated, he signed a federal decree asking government agencies to limit Obamacare-related regulations. The first executive orders signed by Donald Trump are the withdrawal of the United States from the Trans-Pacific Partnership Agreement (TPP), a freeze on the hiring of federal civil servants, an executive order banning funding for international non-governmental organizations that support abortion, the relaunch of two oil pipeline projects, *Keystone XL* (from Canada to the United States), which had been blocked by Barack Obama for environmental reasons, and *Dakota Access* (from North Dakota to Illinois), previously abandoned due to the mobilization of the Standing Rock Sioux tribe and environmental organizations.

On December 2, 2017, the Senate passed a major tax reform bill, designed to lower taxes for corporations and individuals. This is the first major reform of the presidential term of Donald Trump - who had made lower taxes one of his main hobbyhorses - after the failure to repeal Obamacare. Opponents of this massive tax cut argue that it risks benefiting only large corporations and the wealthiest, while penalizing the middle classes and the poorest in the long term. The *New York Times* calls it a "historic tax grab": the newspaper estimates that the reform could increase the US deficit by $1.4 trillion over ten years and, by repealing some of Obamacare's provisions, deprive up to 13 million Americans of health insurance.

Donald Trump is benefiting from a remarkable economic climate. The US economy grew at a stronger-than-expected 3% annualized rate in the third quarter of 2017. Despite his desire to focus on job creation in the United States, the unemployment rate falls sharply and stock market indices reach record highs. The Dow Jones climbed 30% in early 2018, and blue-collar wages rose for the first time in a long time. The favorable economic situation continues throughout 2018: companies, big winners from tax reform, invest at a high rate. In September 2018, unemployment fell to its lowest level since 1969 (3.7%). Trump boasted in November 2017 that he had created 1.65 million private-sector jobs since his election. The number of jobs created, while significant, is nonetheless lower than in the last 11 months of Barack Obama's term. Public spending and the budget deficit continue to rise, however, and real estate investment is on the decline. Donald Trump is pleased with his results, but regrets that the media are not giving them enough coverage. CNN, while acknowledging Donald Trump's credit for the economy's good health, reports that the results do not sufficiently benefit the working classes - on the contrary, tax reform risks increasing inequality - and that the explosion in public deficits is a portent of future problems.

Internationally, Donald Trump is taking a protectionist turn. On January 23, 2017, he announced the withdrawal of the United States from the Trans-Pacific Partnership agreement, which he described as a treaty designed to benefit China. Commentators point out that this free-trade agreement had, on the contrary, been designed by Barack Obama to counterbalance Beijing's influence in Asia, and that the American withdrawal risks giving China a freer hand in the region. In 2017, he launched a renegotiation of the North American Free Trade Agreement. The new agreement, which came into force on October 1, 2018, includes provisions designed to protect the American automotive industry.

In 2018, he launched a series of "trade wars" targeting China, but also the European Union and other countries such as Canada. In January, he introduced four-year tariffs on washing machines and solar panels, of which China is a major exporter. In March, he announced taxes of 25% on steel imports and 10% on aluminum. In disagreement with this policy, Gary Cohn, the President's chief economic advisor, resigned. Further taxes on Chinese products were introduced during the year, while Beijing retaliated by taxing American products. Trump's trade policy raises tensions with U.S. allies: in June 2018, at the close of the G7 summit in Quebec, Canadian Prime Minister Justin Trudeau declares that the new U.S. taxes are "insulting" to Canada. Donald Trump then tweeted that he was disassociating himself from the joint G7 communiqué he had just signed.

Unemployment then continues to fall to 3.6% in April 2019, a level not seen since 1969, mainly due to the number of hires in the business services, health and social assistance sectors.

Immigration

On January 27, 2017, International Holocaust Remembrance Day, he signed an executive order banning refugees of all nationalities from entering the US for 120 days, Iraqi, Iranian, Sudanese, Libyan, Somali and Yemeni nationals for 90 days, and Syrian nationals indefinitely, with the exception of diplomatic visa holders and members of international institutions. The targeted countries are all predominantly Muslim. Faced with the outcry, Donald Trump justified himself by explaining at a press conference that he wanted to protect Americans from "radical Islamist terrorists". However, some media outlets noted an inconsistency in these remarks, since Saudi Arabia, many of whose nationals have carried out attacks on American soil, was not targeted by the decree, probably for economic reasons. In an interview on a Christian channel, he also stressed that, from now on, Christian refugees and other religious minorities in the Middle East would be given priority over Muslim refugees. Iran decides to apply the principle of reciprocity and bans American nationals from entering its territory until Trump's decision is lifted. His decision provokes demonstrations across the US and protests around the world.

The State of Washington announces on January 30, 2017 its intention to file suit against the anti-immigration decree. Several companies headquartered in the state, including Amazon and Expedia, indicate that they will join the suit in the state's federal court.

On January 31, Trump sacked acting Attorney General Sally Yates, after she publicly criticized the anti-immigration executive order and ordered federal prosecutors not to defend it in court.

On February 3, a federal judge in the state of Washington issued a ruling blocking the execution of the anti-immigration decree throughout the United States, in order to allow examination of the complaint filed by the state's attorney general.

At the end of December 2018, his desire to build a protective wall along the US land border, a promise during his presidential campaign, ran into opposition from the newly elected Democratic-dominated Congress. This leads to the longest *shutdown* in U.S. history.

Other aspects

On March 24, 2017, in the absence of a majority to pass the text, Trump was forced to withdraw the health reform bill designed to repeal the social protection legislation, known as "Obamacare". This setback to his flagship campaign promise was unanimously hailed as a major political setback by the American press, which spoke of a "debacle", a "humiliation" and "proof of incompetence". On May 4, in a new vote, the House of Representatives adopted the Obamacare repeal bill. The new health insurance proposal, dubbed "Trumpcare", is then submitted to the Senate for approval: according to a report by the Congressional Budget Office, the text presented could deprive 23 million Americans of health coverage by 2026. In July 2017, two Republican senators announced their intention to vote against the new version of "Trumpcare", making it impossible to secure a majority in Congress for the project. Faced with this new setback, Donald Trump postpones health insurance reform, simply calling on Congress to "abolish Obamacare". At the end of July, a proposal to partially repeal Obamacare was rejected by the Senate.

In September and October 2017, after Hurricane Irma hit Puerto Rico, Donald Trump was widely criticized for the slow pace of relief efforts in the U.S. territory. He reacted by denouncing the management of the crisis by local authorities and calling for a reform of Puerto Rico's infrastructure, while stressing that federal aid to the island would not last forever. His statements continued to fuel controversy, with the mayor of San Juan accusing the president of being "incapable of fulfilling his moral obligation" to help the Puerto Rican people.

Moreover, in the first few months of his presidency, Trump took a series of important social and economic measures: he tightened employee access to retirement accounts, allowed coal companies to dump waste in rivers and exploit natural parks, cancelled the requirement to report methane emissions, and restricted funding for abortion assistance organizations.

In his first year in the White House, Trump has appointed three times as many federal judges as Barack Obama did in the same period. Made at an unusually fast pace, these appointments involve highly conservative figures who, appointed for life, are destined to have a profound influence on American legislation.

In October 2018, the controversial appointment of Brett Kavanaugh swung the Supreme Court to the right, with conservative justices - also appointed for life - becoming the majority. In September 2020, six weeks before the elections, the death of Justice Ruth Bader Ginsburg leaves a vacancy on the Supreme Court (which then has 5 conservative justices and 3 Democratic justices). In order to firmly establish the Court in the conservative camp and, according to the *New York Times,* thus benefit from an ultimate recourse that would be favorable to him if he challenged the elections before the Court, Donald Trump rushed to appoint Amy Coney Barrett, a judge known for her very conservative positions, notably against abortion rights. This shift led to the reversal of Roe v. Wade and Planned Parenthood v. Casey (en).

According to the authors of a 2023 Fondation Jean-Jaurès report on women's rights, "Donald Trump's presidency has been devastating for women's rights in the U.S. and internationally: he has reactivated the Mexico City Policy (en), nicknamed the *Global Gag Rule,* introduced by Ronald Reagan in 1985 and successively repealed by each Democratic administration and reinstated by each Republican administration, which prevents foreign organizations receiving US family planning assistance from performing abortions, providing abortion counseling and information services, or advocating for access to abortion services in their countries, even using non-US funds. Donald Trump has also implemented regulations jeopardizing women's health and gender equality, or cut US funding to the United Nations Population Fund

(UNFPA), which is the largest source of funds for family planning and SRHR in the world.

Covid-19 pandemic

Starting in the spring of 2020, Donald Trump is involved in managing the global Covid-19 epidemic, one of the most serious health crises in American history. He appoints Mike Pence as head of the White House coronavirus *task force*.

Giving daily press conferences, he makes disconcerting statements, such as the possibility of remedies such as disinfectant injections. Relying on the opinions of health personnel, including Chinese doctors, he points the finger of blame at the World Health Organization (WHO) - which had not questioned China's statements - and freezes American participation in its funding. He called on the United Nations to "hold China accountable for its actions" and blamed the Chinese government for the worldwide spread of Covid-19. At first, he refused to wear a mask in public, unlike most other heads of state; he later used one occasionally, notably after the first recommendations from the health authorities, but without imposing it on the population.

On October 2, 2020, a month before the presidential election, Donald Trump announced that he had tested positive for the coronavirus - as had his wife, Melania -

and that he was quarantining himself at the White House. Admitted to hospital the following day, he was discharged after a three-day stay, claiming to be "immune", despite evidence of recontamination in affected patients. Following these remarks, the social network Twitter reduced the visibility of its messages in order to limit the spread of false information about Covid-19.

On November 9, six days after the presidential election, the German laboratory BioNTech and its American partner Pfizer announced that their Covid vaccine candidate was "90% effective". The president's camp sees this as a Trump success, but Trump's involvement is denied by both companies, whose executives the president accuses of delaying the announcement to make him lose. President Trump then seemed "to have lost interest in the pandemic", according to journalist Marc Chalamet, announcing that his administration would not order containment and threatening not to deliver vaccines to the state of New York led by Democrat Andrew Cuomo, accusing him of not believing in the vaccine's reliability.

A few months after his departure from the White House, the possibility of a Chinese laboratory accident that had let the virus escape was raised again when Joe Biden asked for a report on the origin of Covid-19. This thesis, long described as "conspiracy" by international institutions and the mainstream media, was the one put forward by the Trump administration, which blamed the Wuhan Institute of Virology.

Environment

On June 1, 2017, in line with his election platform, he announced the withdrawal of the United States from the Paris climate agreement, without however ruling out re-entering the process after renegotiation, or even concluding a "new agreement that protects" the United States. Furthermore, he does not foresee an exit from the agreement before the end of 2020. A formal US withdrawal will only be possible after November 4, 2020, the day after the presidential election. He justifies his decision by a desire to defend the American economy, based on data deemed misinterpreted or erroneous. This announcement provoked fierce criticism in the United States. It was also condemned by almost all the world's leaders. In August 2017, the United States confirms its presence at the Bonn climate conference.

After promising during the election campaign that coal would remain "king" in the United States, Donald Trump put an end soon after his election to the Clean Power Act, a program designed to encourage electricity producers to reduce their emissions and switch to less polluting energy. The President made a number of other industry-friendly decisions, including appointing an ex-coal lobbyist, Andrew R. Wheeler, to head the Environmental Protection Agency (EPA), and allowing coal producers to dump their waste into waterways. Early in his term, he suspended federal subsidies to the renewable energy sector and, in January 2017, issued executive orders reviving the two controversial oil pipeline projects Keystone XL and Dakota Access, which the Obama administration had been forced to abandon.

In 2017, the US government authorized the slaughter of protected large predators in Alaska (such as grizzly bears and wolves), and opened up a protected area of the same region to oil drilling. It is also taking steps in 2018 to greatly expand offshore drilling in US waters. The Interior Department is proposing to open up almost the entire country's coastline to drilling.

In April 2017, the U.S. president decided to review the status of the 40,000 national monuments designated over the past twenty years. In February 2020, his administration opens the Grand Staircase-Escalante and Bears Ears, located in Utah, to mining and drilling. The former sees the size of its protected area cut by almost half, while the latter loses 85%, the largest elimination of a protected area in U.S. history.

MAKE AMERICA
GREAT AGAIN

Foreign policy

Donald Trump is rapidly imposing his own distinctive style on foreign policy. According to academic Maya Kandel, Donald Trump's intention to "revolutionize American foreign policy", "at the heart of his campaign promises", has resulted in a paradigm shift associated with "the emergence of a new alliance between non-interventionists and nationalists": "strategic competition and, more precisely, 'systemic' rivalry with China has replaced the fight against terrorism as the primary purpose of foreign policy; the page of the extension of market democracies has been turned".

In addition to the Paris climate agreement and the Vienna agreement on Iran's nuclear program, Donald Trump announced the United States' withdrawal from several emblematic bodies or programs: the United Nations Relief and Works Agency for Palestine Refugees in the Near East, the United Nations Human Rights Council, the United Nations Educational, Scientific and Cultural Organization (UNESCO), and the Global Compact for Refugees. It also announces the withdrawal of funding from the United Nations Population Fund.

Donald Trump appoints his strategic advisor Steve Bannon to the *National Security Council*, the decision-making body at the heart of power for national security and foreign policy issues. Bannon, who ran the Breitbart News website, is notably reputed to be a white supremacist.

At the end of May 2017, he embarked on his first diplomatic tour. After stops in Saudi Arabia and Israel, he attended the NATO summit and then the G7 summit, where his style and statements caused tension with the other leaders. The G7 meeting ended without a common position on global warming.

On September 19, 2017, he spoke at the UN to set out his vision of international relations. In a speech of unusual virulence for the venue, peppered with colorful expressions, he returned in particular to the crisis with the Pyongyang regime, saying he was ready to "totally destroy" North Korea in the event of an attack. He also denounces Venezuela's "socialist dictatorship" and declares that the Iran nuclear deal is "one of the worst in which the United States has ever participated". In addition to this diatribe against "rogue states", he points out that American contributions to the UN represent an "unfair financial burden" for the United States, and calls for reform of the institution.

On January 12, 2018, the *Washington Post* reported that the previous day, at a White House meeting dedicated to the protection of immigrants from Haiti, El Salvador and several African nations, Donald Trump reportedly questioned, in the presence of several senators, the value of welcoming so many people from "these *shithole* countries" to the United States, adding that the U.S. should instead bring in more immigrants from countries like Norway. During this discussion, he also reportedly rejected the possibility of an agreement on the protection of Haitian immigrants, declaring: "Why do we need more Haitians? Kick them out". The same day the *Washington Post article was* published, the African group's ambassadors to the United Nations issued a statement condemning the remarks attributed to Donald Trump and demanding a "retraction" and "apology" from him. At first, the White House did not deny the reported remarks. Then, without denying the substance of his remarks, the American president affirmed the following day in a *tweet that* he had not used "this language". The words attributed to Trump triggered an outcry and a wave of indignation around the world: the American president was accused not only of rudeness, but also of racism.

Saudi Arabia

In Saudi Arabia, the first stop on his diplomatic tour in May 2017, he took positions contrary to those of his predecessor, aligning himself with the Saudi vision of the region and denouncing the role of Iran. He then visited Israel, where he affirmed his faith in the Israeli-American alliance, without proposing any specific solution to the

Israeli-Palestinian conflict. Although he had pledged during his campaign to achieve this at the very start of his term of office, he postponed the transfer of the US embassy from Tel Aviv-Jaffa to Jerusalem, which had been called for by both the Israeli right-wing in power and American conservatives, and against which Arab countries were waging a lobbying campaign.

Israeli-Palestinian conflict

On December 6, 2017, claiming a new approach to the Israeli-Palestinian conflict, he officially recognized Jerusalem as Israel's capital and instructed the U.S. embassy to move there. His decision was welcomed by Israeli Prime Minister Benyamin Netanyahu, who declared that Trump's announcement marked a "historic day". Hamas calls on Arab and Muslim countries to expel American ambassadors from their territories.

Russia

As early as January 2017, Donald Trump advocated better understanding with Russia, particularly in the fight against the Islamic State organization. U.S.-Russian relations are, however, traversed by periods of tension, particularly in the context of the war in Syria. In April 2018, Trump wrote in a tweet that US relations with Russia are "worse today than they have ever been, including during the Cold

War", and advocated better understanding between the two countries.

On July 16, 2018, he met Russian President Vladimir Putin at a summit between Russia and the United States in Helsinki. Shortly beforehand, he again deplores the deterioration in Russian-American relations on Twitter and blames it in part on prosecutor Robert Mueller, who has just indicted twelve members of Russian intelligence as part of the investigation into Russia's interference in the US presidential election. Questioned by journalists in Helsinki about this affair, he disavowed his own secret services, declaring that he saw no reason why Russia should have done so. In response to the outcry, he said that his tongue had slipped and that he saw no reason "why Russia shouldn't have done it".

Iran

On May 8, 2018, he made good on his election promise in the 2016 US presidential elections, by withdrawing from the Vienna Agreement on Iran's nuclear program (JCPoA). This decision was strongly criticized by the countries that signed the agreement, but approved by the Middle Eastern countries that are allies of the United States. On May 21, 2018, Mike Pompeo, the US Secretary of State, laid down twelve conditions for any new agreement with Iran, and promised "the toughest sanctions in history" in the event of refusal.

On January 3, 2020, after an attack attributed to pro-Iran militias on the US embassy in Iraq on December 31, 2019, Donald Trump authorized an attack targeting and killing Iranian general Qassem Soleimani.

North Korea

In order to put pressure on the North Korean regime, in response to its nuclear weapons tests and use of ballistic weapons, in April 2017 it announced the dispatch of an "armada" to the Korean peninsula. North Korea said it was "ready for war" and would respond "to any nuclear attack with nuclear force". Trump finally renounced sending a naval air group to North Korea, consisting of the aircraft carrier USS *Carl Vinson* and its squadron.

In early March 2018, several verbal escalations in US-North Korean relations raised fears of a nuclear conflict. However, to everyone's surprise, the North Korean leader proposes a meeting with the American president where, among other things, nuclear-related disputes would be negotiated. Donald Trump accepted the invitation. The meeting is scheduled for June 12, 2018 in Singapore, but is cancelled by Trump in May due to the return of North Korea's bellicose rhetoric and the North Korean government's rejection of the US administration's denuclearization demands. A few days later, following a conciliatory statement from North Korea, the meeting was held as planned. The meeting was welcomed by the international community.

Donald Trump continues to exchange views with Kim Jong-un. On June 30, 2019, he enters Panmunjeom alongside the North Korean leader. This was a historic first, as no American president had ever before entered North Korea. On this occasion, the two leaders reaffirmed their determination to relaunch the country's denuclearization process.

Mexico

In the midst of diplomatic tension between the United States and Mexico, he denounced on Twitter the US trade deficit with the neighboring country and the Mexican government's refusal to pay for the separation wall between the two countries, prompting the cancellation of his meeting with President Peña Nieto.

On January 25, 2017, he signed an executive order kicking off construction of the Mexican border wall he had promised during his campaign.

Syria

On April 7, 2017, in the wake of the Khan Cheikhoun chemical attack committed by the Syrian army, he ordered the bombing of the Al-Chaayrate air base. In mid-May 2017, he provokes controversy by revealing, during a meeting at the White House with Russian Foreign Minister Sergei Lavrov, information deemed confidential about operations carried out by an "allied country" against the Islamic State organization. On June 12, 2017, the *New York Times* revealed that it was an operation by "Israeli hackers who had penetrated a small cell of Daesh terrorists in Syria. It was thanks to this infiltration and the sharing of information gathered that US intelligence learned that the terrorist group was working on explosives capable of fooling airport X-ray scanners by making them look exactly like laptop batteries. In March, the U.S. Department of Homeland Security had announced a cabin ban on electronic devices for U.S.-bound travelers from airports in Egypt, Jordan, Kuwait, Morocco, Qatar, Saudi Arabia, Turkey and the United Arab Emirates.

On December 19, 2018, he created a surprise - including within his own administration - by announcing the withdrawal of US troops from Syria. He justifies this decision on the grounds that the Islamic State has been "defeated", which in his view makes a US military presence unnecessary. In particular, this American withdrawal would result in the abandonment of local Kurdish-dominated forces, supported by the West but considered enemies by Turkey, and would also play into the hands of Bashar al-Assad's regime. Defense Secretary

James Mattis disagreed with this decision and resigned the following day.

On October 27, 2019, in a televised address, he announced the death of the leader of the Islamic State, Abu Bakr al-Baghdadi, during a military operation carried out by US special forces in Syria: fleeing from the soldiers, the latter died by detonating his explosives belt, also killing three of his children. These conditions prompted Donald Trump to say that "this brute spent his last hours in panic, fear and terror, terrified by the American force bearing down on him", that "he died like a dog, like a coward" and that "the world is now a safer place".

Controversies

Accusations of conflicts of interest

The *Washington Post*'s November 2016 analysis of Donald Trump's asset declarations reveals that at least 111 Trump-owned companies have done business in eighteen countries and territories across South America, Asia and the Middle East, some in countries with which the US has sensitive financial or diplomatic relations, such as Saudi Arabia, Turkey, the United Arab Emirates, China, Israel, Azerbaijan, Indonesia or Panama.

Despite the significant risk of these business links becoming sources of conflicts of interest, Trump announced his refusal to sell his assets or entrust them to an independent manager before entering the White House, contrary to the tradition followed by most of the last American presidents, from Reagan to Bush, preferring to commit to leaving the management of his companies to his children and executives.

This unprecedented situation places Trump's conglomerate in a position unprecedented in American presidential history, both as a possible conduit for intermediaries seeking favors from the presidency, and as a potential target for attacks or threats abroad. Yet Donald Trump himself acknowledges as "a small conflict of interest" the $10 million contract concluded in 2014 with the Turkish consortium Doğan Holding, which has since become an influential supporter of the repressive regime in Ankara. Ethics advisors see the contract more as a personal source of income that could expose Trump to foreign influence and sway his decision-making as chief executive.

On the other hand, many of Trump's real estate projects and properties are backed by loans from major foreign banks, some of them German or Chinese, such as the Bank of China, which Trump has regularly criticized. Deutsche Bank, Trump's biggest creditor, is currently negotiating a multi-billion-dollar settlement for abuses linked to the subprime crisis. Negotiations for this penalty are being conducted with the Department of Justice, which will soon be headed by officials appointed by Donald Trump.

The question of Trump's overseas holdings remains unresolved, as he has refused to allow a financial audit of his investments, as well as to provide certain documents such as his tax returns, which would provide greater insight into his overseas accounts.

On December 24, 2016, Trump announced his intention to dissolve his foundation to "avoid even the appearance of a conflict of interest". However, this announcement has virtually no impact, as his foundation is already de facto inactive by order of the American courts. What's more, such a decision would do nothing to change Trump's capital links with the hundreds of companies that make up his "opaque, unlisted" conglomerate.

On January 11, 2017, Donald Trump announced measures to prevent potential conflicts of interest, including placing the Trump Organization under the control of a trust run by two of his sons. Walter Shaub, director of the U.S. Office of Government Ethics, details this plan at length at a conference, deeming it "totally inadequate" and declaring that it "does not meet the standards followed by his cabinet appointees, nor by every president for four decades". Walter Shaub recalls the recommendations made to Donald Trump by the bureau: "He must give up his shares. Nothing else will resolve these conflicts".

On March 9, 2017, the Trademark Office of China's State Administration for Commerce and Industry gave its prior approval for the registration of 38 trademarks related to Donald Trump, protecting the intellectual property rights of the US president and his family in China. Following the example of Senator Ben Cardin, a member of the Senate Foreign Relations Committee, many Democratic senators and legal experts believe that China's agreement on the "Trump brand" can be considered a form of benefit granted by a foreign government, which the US Constitution prohibits for a sitting president. In response to this accusation of a conflict of interest, the Trump Organization's head of legal affairs states that the group had been seeking to protect its rights in China for some ten years already. However, the application to register these trademarks was filed in April 2016 by Donald Trump's lawyers, mostly in the name of "Donald J. Trump".

On June 12, 2017, the attorneys general of Maryland and the District of Columbia filed a complaint against President Trump, considering that he was at the center of an "unprecedented violation of the Constitution". A similar complaint had been filed on the previous January 23 by Citizens for Responsibility and Ethics in Washington (en).

On June 14, 2017, 196 Democratic Senators and Representatives in Congress filed a complaint based on Article I, Section 9, Clause 8 of the U.S. Constitution, known as the Foreign Emoluments Clause or the Nobility Titles Clause. This clause prohibits any person holding public office from "accepting any gift, emolument, office, or title of any kind from any king, prince, or foreign state" without the consent of Congress. In their complaint, these elected officials point out that this clause "was enacted to ensure that our nation's leaders would not be corrupted by foreign influence or place their special financial interests ahead of the national interest", and that the lack of a clear cut between Trump and his companies places him in a permanent conflict of interest.

On March 28, 2018, a federal court in Maryland declared admissible the complaint filed in June 2017 by the attorneys general of Maryland and the District of Columbia. In his decision, the federal judge states that "Plaintiffs have sufficiently alleged that the President is violating the Foreign and Domestic Emoluments Clauses of the Constitution due to his involvement and receipt of profits from the Trump International Hotel and its outbuildings in Washington, as well as the Trump Organization's operations in this matter." In particular, he refers to "an actual injury, clearly linked to the President's actions, and an injury that can be redressed by the court". The investigation of this complaint could be the start of a long legal battle, as the Democratic communities intend to demand Donald Trump's tax returns, which he has always refused to make public.

Alleged links

On January 12, 2018, the *Wall Street Journal* claims that pornographic film actress Stormy Daniels received $130,000 just before the presidential election, in exchange for her silence regarding a sexual relationship she allegedly had with Donald Trump in 2006, when his wife Melania was pregnant with their son Barron. On February 13, the president's personal lawyer confirmed that the sum had indeed been paid. At the beginning of March, the pornographic actress filed a complaint to invalidate the confidentiality clause linked to the $130,000 payment. Trump's lawyers announced that they would be claiming $20 million from Stormy Daniels for breach of the agreement.

On March 20, 2018, former playmate Karen McDougal filed suit in her turn to invalidate a confidentiality clause concerning the affair she allegedly had with Donald Trump. The actress and model claims to have received $150,000, half of which was allegedly paid to her lawyer in agreement with Trump. On March 25, 2018, Stormy Daniels gave an interview to CBS in which she recounted in detail her relationship with Donald Trump, who at the time allegedly lured her to appear on *The Celebrity Apprentice*. She also claims that Trump's entourage threatened her to dissuade her from speaking out. In September 2018, she published a book telling her side of the story. Donald Trump, for his part, categorically denies having had an affair with the actress.

On December 12, 2018, Michael Cohen, Donald Trump's former personal lawyer, was sentenced to three years in prison for having, during his client's presidential campaign, bought the silence of Stormy Daniels and Karen McDougal by paying $130,000 to the former and $150,000 to the latter.

Media relations

Beginning with the 2016 election, *The Washington Post, The New York Times* and many political commentators drew parallels between Donald Trump's rise and that of Adolf Hitler.

These critics point out the similarities between the two men's rhetoric, slogans and political methods, and note the similarities between historical situations, publicly expressing concern about the danger they see threatening American democracy.

In an article for Le *Monde*, World War II historian Robert Paxton acknowledges that the temptation to describe the newly-elected president as a "fascist" may be strong, given his authoritarian personality and the typically fascist motives he adopts: "deploring national decline, blaming it on foreigners and minorities; disregard for legal rules; implicit endorsement of violence against opponents; rejection of everything international, be it trade, institutions or existing treaties". For Paxton, however, "executive power without constraint or control is indicative of dictatorship in general, rather than fascism in particular". He believes that the "fascist" label obscures the pro-rich economic and social libertarianism of the Trump regime, which he prefers to describe as a "plutocracy". In *Foreign Policy*, historian and academic Eliah Bures points out that most American presidents have been described as fascists since the 1970s, and believes that Donald Trump cannot be classified as such.

Following his inauguration, Donald Trump continues to make regular use of social networks, which he sees as a means of addressing citizens directly without going through the channels or supposed censorship of the media. The official White House and presidential Twitter account, @Potus, is administered by Deputy Communications Director Dan Scavino. Donald Trump nevertheless continues to communicate with his personal Twitter account, @RealDonaldTrump, which is much more active than the presidential account. He uses it in the same way as during his campaign, notably to criticize the actions of his opponents and the media, as well as to remind people of his agenda. Highly reactive on Twitter, he expresses himself "unfiltered", often using emotional, even invective, language. Tweets can also have a diplomatic impact: Donald Trump has provoked reactions from the Chinese authorities, for example, by writing very directly about his views on China's trade and military policies.

Between January and April 2017, Harvard University's Shorenstein (en) Center on Media and Politics examined what journalists from ten major media outlets published in print about Donald Trump during the first hundred days of his presidency. From this study, it emerges that:

- Trump dominates media coverage. He is the subject of 41% of all news stories (three times more than previous US presidents).
- His ability to preside is questioned more often in Europe than in the United States.
- News coverage sets a new standard for negative press. Not a single media outlet is more positive than negative.
- Overall, the tone is negative in 80% of news items (57% negative for George W. Bush, 60% for Bill Clinton).
- The negative tone is 93% for CNN and NBC, 91% for CBS, 87% for the *New York Times*, 83% for the *Washington Post*, 70% for *The Wall Street Journal*, 52% for Fox News; in Europe, the negative tone reaches a record 98% for ARD, 84% for the *Financial Times* and 74% for the BBC.
- The three subjects least contested by journalists are the economy (54% negative tone), the terrorist threat (70%) and other domestic political affairs (72%).

Commenting on this study, several media outlets point out that a negative tone does not mean that the treatment of information is biased. Commenting on this study, the *Washington Post* further points out that "when you do controversial things - and polls show that a huge amount of the things Trump does are controversial - you find yourself criticized by some people. And when you promise to do extraordinary things and the results contradict your promises, it's hard to cover that up as a victory."

During his campaign and after taking office, Donald Trump maintained a highly confrontational relationship with the mass media, which he accused of being biased against him. He declares that he has "an ongoing war with the media" and, in his tweets and various interventions, goes so far as to insult journalists as a whole, calling them "the most dishonest human beings in the world", "liars", "impostors", "scum", etc.... On June 26, 2017, three CNN journalists were forced to resign for publishing an article that included inaccurate information about links between a member of Donald Trump's entourage and Russian financial circles. The president reacted by denouncing all the "fake news" published on his account by various major American media. A few days later, he retweeted a video montage showing him punching a figure bearing the CNN logo for a head. The violence of the polemics between the White House and the media reached an unprecedented level, which *Le Monde* summed up as "an unprecedented battle of words and invective". As well as regularly reacting to Trump's attacks, including with scoops and revelations, the American media are also profiting economically: coverage of the Trump presidency by TV channels is enabling them to record audience peaks.

During 2018, his relationship continued to deteriorate with the mainstream American media, which he regularly referred to as "*fake news*", and "real enemies of the people" in response to the strong criticism raised after his meeting with Vladimir Putin in Helsinki. In July of this year, Arthur Gregg Sulzberger, editor of the *New York Times*, one of the media outlets most fiercely attacked by Donald Trump, confirmed that he had met with the president at the White House, at the latter's request. During these exchanges, A. G. Sulzberger says he warned the president "that this inflammatory language was contributing to an increase in threats against journalists and would incite violence", and that he "implored him to reverse his disproportionate attacks on journalism, which I believe are dangerous and harmful to our country". On the following August 16, over 350 local and national American newspapers, websites and magazines, both progressive and conservative, published editorials reaffirming their right to inform in the face of the President's attacks, and insisting on the importance of media independence.

According to an academic poll of 170 historians and political scientists conducted in early 2018, he is ranked the worst president in U.S. history.

Like his presidential campaign, his tenure has been characterized by a large number of lies and approximations, particularly on his Twitter account. At the end of April 2019, in just over two years in office, 10,111 inaccurate statements were noted by the *Washington Post*, an average of 12 "false or misleading words" per day. After three years in office, the same newspaper's fact-checking service announces more than 16,200 "false or misleading" reports, with the average rising to 22 per day in 2019.

Many observers note that Trump's presidency has profoundly disrupted and cleaved the media world.

"Russiagate

"*Russiagate*" overshadowed the first part of the Republican president's term without bringing to light any solid evidence of collusion between Russia and Donald Trump.

On February 13, 2017, Donald Trump was forced to resign his National Security Advisor, Michael T. Flynn. The latter is suspected of having lied - notably to Vice President Mike Pence - about the nature of his December 2016 telephone conversations with the Russian ambassador to the United States, and of being potentially vulnerable to Russian blackmail. On March 2, 2017, in the face of criticism following press revelations about his contacts with the Russian ambassador, Jeff Sessions, U.S. Attorney General, announced that he would recuse himself from any investigation into alleged Russian interference in the presidential election. A February 15, 2017 *New York Times* article indicates that prior to his election to the White House, members of Trump's campaign team, including Paul Manafort, had repeated contacts with senior Russian intelligence officials. According to the daily, US intelligence agencies are reportedly investigating whether members of Donald Trump's team colluded with the Russians to influence the course of the election.

On May 9, 2017, Donald Trump dismissed FBI Director James Comey, then in charge of the investigation into his campaign team's possible collusion with Russia. On June 8, in testimony before the Senate Judiciary Committee, James Comey claims "to have been pressured" and asserts that the president sacked him in order to "change the way the Russia investigation was being conducted" without providing evidence of this. Donald Trump's lawyers announce that they are filing a complaint against Comey for disclosing confidential information, and the president accuses Comey of "lying during his hearing before Congress". Before testifying in his turn, Jeff Sessions declares that he did not fail to declare a meeting with the Russian ambassador and denies the allegations of collusion between Moscow and Donald Trump's campaign team, calling them "a detestable and appalling lie".

In March 2019, at the end of a two-year investigation, Special Prosecutor Robert Mueller states in his report that he had not found sufficient evidence to indict an individual from the Trump campaign for conspiracy, but that he did find a dozen possible cases of obstruction of justice.

In November 2021, Special Prosecutor John Durham's investigation cast considerable doubt on the accusations of collusion between Moscow and the former US President, particularly after the arrest and indictment on November 4, 2021 of Igor Danchenko, the main informant in the "Steele dossier" at the root of Russiagate, charged with five counts of lying to the FBI. The informant is accused of having lied and obtained his information from a close associate of the Clintons, Charles Dolan, a public relations advisor to several Democratic campaigns.

John Durham's report, published in May 2023, highlights weaknesses in the FBI's Russiagate investigation and finds that the federal police "lacked objectivity" in analyzing links between Moscow and Donald Trump's 2016 presidential campaign.

Controversial conversation with Zelensky and first impeachment proceedings

In September 2019, Nancy Pelosi, Speaker of the House of Representatives, launched *impeachment* proceedings against him after a whistleblower from the US intelligence community revealed the contents of a telephone conversation in which the US President asked Ukrainian President Volodymyr Zelensky to trigger an investigation into Hunter Biden, son of Joe Biden, a potential Democratic candidate in the 2020 US presidential election.

The Democrat-dominated House of Representatives indicted him for "abuse of power" and "obstruction of Congress", making him the third American president to be indicted, after Andrew Johnson and Bill Clinton. The Republican-majority Senate acquitted him after a two-week trial on February 5, 2020.

cliffhanger

2020 presidential election

Announcement of candidacy

Donald Trump quickly announced his intention to run for a second term, and in January 2017 unveiled the slogan he would use for his campaign: "*Keep America great!*", resonating with his 2016 slogan, "*Make America Great Again*". He also appoints a campaign manager, Brad Parscale, who previously worked for him in the 2016 campaign. He confirms that he wants Mike Pence to serve a second term as Vice President.

Republican nomination

He officially launches his presidential campaign on June 18, 2019, from Orlando, Florida, alongside Mike Pence and Melania Trump. In the Republican primaries, he is challenged by Bill Weld and Joe Walsh. He easily won all the ballots cast (with over 90% of the vote) and secured enough delegates to be nominated again as the Republican Party's candidate on March 17, 2020. He is nominated as the party's candidate at the convention on August 24, 2020.

General election

As in 2016, polls show him well ahead of his Democratic opponent in voting intentions nationally and in most key states.

The Covid-19 pandemic forced him to suspend his campaign for several weeks.

At the first televised debate on September 29, 2020 in Cleveland, he showed great aggression towards his Democratic opponent Joe Biden, to the point that some American commentators called the encounter "the worst debate in history". Donald Trump calls on the neo-fascist militia group Proud Boys to "stand down and be ready", adding that "somebody's got to do something about these antifas and the left. It's not a right-wing problem. It's the left. He also threatens to challenge any defeat in the Supreme Court.

On October 2, 2020, a month before the presidential election and a few days after a meeting that provoked a cluster, Donald Trump, then aged 74, announced that he and his wife Melania were suffering from Covid-19 and immediately quarantined himself at the White House, suspending his scheduled campaign rallies. The President's personal physician declared that he had only "mild symptoms, but remains in good spirits". He received an experimental synthetic antibody treatment developed by Regeneron. Donald Trump was admitted to Walter Reed Military Hospital on the evening of October 2. Suffering from "fever and fatigue", the President is expected to remain hospitalized for "a few days as a precaution". The White House Chief of Staff says the president will continue to perform his duties from the hospital's presidential apartments. Should Donald Trump be prevented from performing his duties, Vice President Mike Pence would temporarily replace him in office during his inability to govern. He returned to the White House after three days in hospital and once again defended his criticized handling of the pandemic.

Cured of Covid-19, Donald Trump immediately resumed his campaign and held a particularly large series of public meetings while the pandemic was still ongoing. A study by Stanford University estimates that all these meetings resulted in over 30,000 Covid-19 infections and around 700 deaths.

Ahead of the election, Donald Trump and the Republican Party warn of the risk of fraud in his opponent's favor due to the historically high use of absentee and early voting as a result of the Covid-19 pandemic.

On election night on November 2, 2020, as predicted by the incumbent president before the vote and while most polls predicted a landslide victory for Joe Biden, no candidate won enough electoral votes to be declared the winner. Even so, it was announced on election night that Donald Trump had won Florida and Ohio, traditionally the most hotly contested states in recent presidential elections. However, absentee and advance voting are slowing down the counting process in the states where the results are closest, namely Arizona, North Carolina, Georgia, Michigan, Nevada, Pennsylvania and Wisconsin.

A few days later, on November 7, 2020, projections by various media outlets (CNN, Fox News, *The New York Times*) awarded the Democratic candidate Wisconsin, Michigan and finally Pennsylvania, former Democratic strongholds that the outgoing president had managed to swing to the Republican camp in 2016. After two attempts to reach the White House, 77-year-old Joe Biden was elected 46th President of the United States. Donald Trump thus enters the very closed circle of American presidents to have served a single term, since since the Second World War, only Jimmy Carter and George H. W. Bush have been defeated before him. He becomes the first American president whose popularity rating has never exceeded the 50% mark in Gallup polls, who was elected ahead of the popular vote and who has been the subject of impeachment proceedings.

Contesting the result

Donald Trump refuses to acknowledge his defeat, announces that he has largely won the election and denounces massive fraud, without providing any tangible evidence to support his allegations. He multiplies false information, much of which is reported as misleading by Twitter. Donald Trump, his campaign team and his personal lawyer Rudy Giuliani initiated numerous legal proceedings in all the major states that sealed his defeat, but the lack of evidence of possible fraud led to the failure of many complaints filed with local judges. Two weeks after the announcement of Joe Biden's victory, Donald Trump continues to cry massive fraud and tries to intervene in the vote certification procedures, In particular, he put pressure on Republican legislators in Michigan (a state Biden won by more than 150,000 votes) (Joe Biden was elected by the electors on December 14, 2020, and this vote was confirmed by Congress on January 7, 2021), with the idea that, in the absence of certification, it would be up to them to designate the electors themselves, who could then vote in favor of Trump. On November 23, with Joe Biden's victory in Michigan certified, the General Services Administration headed by Emily Murphy launched the presidential transition procedure that had been blocked until then. Donald Trump himself gives credence to these facts, while continuing to cry mass fraud.

On December 14, the Electoral College met and elected Joe Biden as President of the United States, with a final score of 306 electors to Donald Trump's 232.

Nevertheless, the legal and communications battle continued: encouraged by Trump, some Republican senators announced that they would contest the result at the official vote count, scheduled for January 6. Those who were too quick to endorse Biden's victory were threatened by Trump. In all his public speeches during this period leading up to the January 6 assault on Congress gathered on Capitol Hill, he repeats hundreds of times that he has "achieved a landslide victory", uses the words *rigged*, *fraud*, and *fight just* as many times, to "save" or "take back" "our country".

Although Donald Trump received seven million fewer votes than his opponent, the American electoral system is such that he could have been re-elected if he had "flipped" 32,507 votes in four key states. For several decades now, the Electoral College system has favored less populous, often conservative, states: as a result, in the last seven elections, Republican candidates have won three presidential mandates, even though they have been outspent six times by the Democrats in the popular vote. According to election expert Nate Silver, a Democratic candidate needs to score two to three points higher than his or her Republican opponent to have the same chance of being elected.

Invasion of the Capitol

Beginning in December, Donald Trump, with numerous tweets, invited his supporters to demonstrate across the country and to take part, on January 6, 2021, in a huge rally in front of the White House when the final stage of the 2020 electoral process took place on Capitol Hill: congressional certification of the Electoral College votes and Joe Biden's victory, in order to challenge it. At the rally, he declared to his thousands of supporters: "Our country has had enough. We can't take it anymore. And to use the favorite term that brought you here, we're going to stop the theft. You will never take back our country with weakness. You must show strength and you must be strong. You have to *fight* like hell. If you don't fight like hell, you won't have a country. Everyone here will soon march to the Capitol [where the certification of the presidential election results takes place], to peacefully and patriotically make your voices heard" (the word "peacefully" being uttered only once in an hour's speech). Shortly afterwards, the storming of the Capitol by hundreds of his supporters, seen as an insurrection or attempted coup d'état, provoked strong reactions against him at home and abroad, and calls for his impeachment. Donald Trump appeared particularly isolated, with the loss of some support in the Republican camp and the threat of a new impeachment procedure by the Democrats. Some of his ministers resigned (the Secretaries of State for Transport and Education, the

Minister of Health), while several Democrats, including Congresswoman Nancy Pelosi, asked Mike Pence to invoke the 25th Amendment of the Constitution to declare President Trump unfit to govern, which he refused to do. A YouGov poll indicates that, while a majority of Americans see the attack as a threat to democracy, 45% of Republican voters favor the initiative.

Donald Trump released a video the following evening in which he condemned the assault and violence. He claims that he "immediately deployed National Guard and federal forces to secure the building and evict intruders", promises to make "those who broke the law" pay, and calls on his supporters to "go home". Acting on his defeat, but reiterating his accusations of fraud, he asserts that he wanted to "protect American democracy" by using legal means to contest the election results, promises a "smooth transition of power" and calls for "reconciliation" after Congressional certification. This sudden turnaround, dictated by circumstances, is designed to respond to criticism from within his own camp. Donald Trump is thus attempting to correct the disastrous impression left by the video broadcast the day before, in which he repeated his allegations of fraud and a "stolen" election, and invited the rioters to "go home", while assuring them that he understood them and expressed his affection for them: "*We love you, you're very special*".

Eviction from social networks

On January 8, 2021, Twitter permanently closes his account, which was followed by over 88 million people, "due to a risk of inciting violence". His Facebook and Instagram accounts are also closed "until further notice". This decision by social networks to close or suspend the account of a sitting head of state is a world first, sparking heated debate in the United States and around the world. Mexican President Andrés Manuel López Obrador questioned "freedom and the right to information" and "the role of legally and legitimately constituted authorities", while whistleblower Edward Snowden spoke of a "turning point in the battle for control of information". On the other hand, for some on the American left, this decision comes too late.

Twitch, Snapchat and YouTube are also shutting down official Donald Trump accounts indefinitely. Chinese social media outlet TikTok, which Donald Trump's administration wanted to ban in July 2020, is removing videos of the president's speeches as well as certain keywords and hashtags referring to the "patriotic party". For its part, Shopify is withdrawing sales from official Donald Trump sites such as *Make America Great Again* caps.

Donald Trump's Twitter account was finally reactivated on November 20, 2022, after the platform's new owner, billionaire Elon Musk, conducted a poll on his own Twitter account the previous day entitled "Should former President Trump be reinstated?".

Second impeachment procedure

In the wake of the Capitol Hill invasion, several Democratic lawmakers are considering launching impeachment proceedings against Donald Trump on January 11. If successful, this procedure would not only have symbolic consequences, but could also render Donald Trump ineligible and thus prevent him from running in the 2024 presidential election.

On January 13, the House of Representatives approved Donald Trump's impeachment for "inciting insurrection" by 232 votes (including 10 Republicans) to 197. Among the members of the president's party who voted to impeach him was Liz Cheney, third highest among Republican representatives, who said of the riot, "There has never been a greater betrayal by a president." Trump is thus the first president in US history to be impeached twice.

On January 18, the Gallup Institute published the results of an opinion poll, which showed 34% of favorable opinions in his favor. Trump has never exceeded the symbolic 50% mark of favorable intentions during his term in office (he was at 49% before the Covid pandemic).

He is the first president in this situation since this institute began polling in 1938.

Donald Trump will finally be acquitted by the Senate on February 13.

Last televised address to the nation

On January 15, 2021, admitting Joe Biden's victory but refusing to congratulate him, Donald Trump announced that he would leave the White House on the morning of January 20 aboard Marine One, to avoid running into Joe Biden and his teams, and thus avoid any transfer of power. Specialists have noted Trump's destruction of presidential archives, as confirmed by internal testimonies. On January 19, Donald Trump addressed the nation for the last time as president in office. In his speech, he declared, among other things, "As I conclude my term as 45 President of the United States, I stand before you truly proud of what we have accomplished together. We have done what we came here to do and much more. This week, we inaugurate a new administration and pray that it succeeds in ensuring America's security and prosperity." Donald Trump then took his final bow to the American people, saying: "I leave this majestic place with a loyal and joyful heart, an optimistic spirit and a supreme confidence that for our country and for our children, the best is yet to come. Being your President has been the greatest honor of my life. Thank you and farewell. God bless you, God bless the United States of America". He never mentioned the name of his successor in this final address to the nation.

In the final days of his term, Donald Trump proposed a list of one hundred people to be pardoned. Among them are many close friends and collaborators of all kinds: family members, senior civil servants and rappers. These lists were not necessarily validated. Finally, on January 19, he pardoned 73 people, including Steve Bannon, but no one from his family, nor himself.

Leaving the White House

Contrary to tradition, Donald Trump did not attend the swearing-in of his successor, a first since Andrew Johnson in 1869. On January 20, the outgoing president leaves the White House aboard Marine One for Andrews Air Force Base. On arrival at the base, cannon shots are fired, and the President delivers a final speech, in which he declares: "Goodbye, we love you. We'll be back in one form or another. Have a good life, we'll see you soon, farewell". At 9 a.m., the 45th President of the United States takes off for the last time aboard Air Force One, bound for Palm Beach, Florida. Donald Trump and his wife then settle into their private club at Mar-a-Lago. Donald Trump's term ends at noon, when Joe Biden takes the oath of office on the Bible in front of the Capitol, officially becoming the 46th President of the United States.

Legal proceedings subsequent to the president's term of office

Acquittal in the Senate

On February 9, 2021, Donald Trump's impeachment trial begins in the Senate. As he can no longer be impeached, having left office, a conviction could result in a lifetime ban from holding any political office in the United States.

Elected Democrats, relying on a series of videos, accuse Trump of being the "chief instigator" of the Capitol invasion. Elected Republicans reject impeachment proceedings on the grounds that it is unconstitutional to try a former president, arguing that impeachment applies only to sitting federal agents. Trump's defense is led by attorneys Michael van der Veen, David Schoen and Bruce Castor; Bruce Castor's plea elicits jeers from the Democratic camp and dismay from Trump himself.

On February 13, Donald Trump was acquitted by the Senate. Fifty-seven senators voted for a guilty verdict, including seven Republicans, and 43 against, falling ten votes short of the two-thirds majority required by the Constitution. Never before in the history of *impeachment* proceedings in the United States have so many Senators voted in favor of the President's impeachment. Republican Minority Leader Mitch McConnell, who voted "not guilty", explained his reasons: he felt it was not the role of the Senate to impeach a "private citizen"; on the other hand, he considered Donald Trump fully responsible for the way events unfolded, for his lie about the fraudulent assault on January 6, and indicated that it was up to the US justice system to take up his case. For his part, the former president declares, in a statement: "Our magnificent, historic and patriotic movement, *Make America Great Again*, has only just begun".

Parliamentary inquiry into the Capitol assault

On February 2, 2021, Democratic prosecutors referred to the speeches prior to the Capitol invasion as "treason of historic proportions". Trump's lawyers argue that the proceedings are unconstitutional, given his departure from the White House.

On December 19, 2022, the parliamentary commission of inquiry into the Capitol assault issued its findings and recommended that the Department of Justice bring criminal charges against Donald Trump for his role in the event. It believes that the former US president could be charged on four counts: obstruction of official process, conspiracy against the United States, conspiracy to make false statements and inciting or aiding insurrection.

Reactivation and new legal proceedings

Several lawsuits are being reactivated as of January 20, in particular accusations of fraud and sexual assault. The cases in question relate to the financing of the 2016 presidential campaign, the Trump Organization's tax returns, his relationship with pornographic actress Stormy Daniels, and several accusations of sexual assault.

In February 2021, in an investigation into possible tax and banking fraud, the Manhattan district attorney announced that he was examining documents covering 2011 to 2018. This represents several million pages.

On the night of August 8, 2022, the FBI raided Donald Trump's Mar-a-Lago residence in Florida. According to the *Washington Post*, the Secret Service was looking for classified documents that the former president is suspected of having kept after leaving the White House, violating a federal law on espionage in the United States. Donald Trump himself announced that a "raid" by the Secret Service had taken place and denounced a "political persecution". A few days later, the FBI announced that it had found secret documents in the former head of state's residence, some of which concerned the "President of the French Republic". In an unusual press conference, Attorney General Merrick Garland claims to have "personally approved" the search; he condemns the "unfounded attacks" by Republicans against his department and the federal police.

In March 2023, Trump was indicted by a grand jury in Manhattan, New York. He is accused of having charged to legal expenses a sum of $130,000 paid to Stormy Daniels to keep her quiet about the extramarital relationship he allegedly had with her in 2006. Trump would therefore have broken electoral law by falsifying this accounting. He is the first former American president in history to be the subject of a criminal prosecution. On April 4, 2023, formally placed under arrest, Donald Trump pleaded not guilty to the thirty-four charges against him. He denounced political persecution in the run-up to the 2024 presidential election, pointed out that the prosecutor was a Democrat and denounced the alleged weaknesses of his legal arguments.

Indictments linked to his attempts to stay in power

On August 1, 2023, Special Prosecutor Jack Smith, appointed by the Department of Justice, announces the indictment of Donald Trump on charges of "conspiracy against the United States", for what is described as an "unprecedented assault on American democracy" in connection with his attempts to retain power after his defeat in the 2020 presidential elections and the Assault on the Capitol. 15 days later, the state of Georgia, where pressure from Trump and his allies had been particularly strong, indicted him and eighteen co-defendants on charges including "false statements and documents, usurpation of public office, forgery and pressure on witnesses....".

Persistent influence at national level

The former president made his first major appearance since leaving the White House on February 28, 2021, speaking at the Conservative Political Action Conference, where he raised the possibility of running again for a second term, repeating that he might "decide to beat the Democrats a third time". Analysts believed that he was as influential as ever in the Republican Party, and that his popularity there remained intact despite the events on Capitol Hill in January. Opinion polls show him as the clear favorite for the 2024 Republican primaries.

Joe Biden requests on February 5, 2021 that Donald Trump not have access to intelligence briefings. While former presidents traditionally enjoy such access, Biden believes Trump "doesn't need to receive intelligence briefings". He says: "What sense does it make to give him an intelligence briefing? What impact does it have anymore, beyond the fact that he might slip up and say something?".

Still suspended from Twitter and Facebook, Trump launches and uses his blog, "From The Desk of Donald Trump", which operates similarly to Twitter, in May and June 2021, when he closes it. At the same time, it was announced that his Facebook and Instagram accounts would be suspended for a minimum of two years, until the "risks to public safety have disappeared", leading Donald Trump to speak of "an insult" to his "75 million voters" in the 2020 presidential election.

On June 26, 2021, in Wellington, Ohio, the former president held a rally for the first time since leaving the White House. There, he portrayed Democrats as "radical leftists" responsible for an upsurge in violent crime, described the Biden administration as "a disaster" and reiterated his baseless accusations of fraud in the 2020 presidential election.

In October 2021, as polls continued to give him a tie with Joe Biden in the event of a 2024 presidential bid, Donald Trump announced the launch of his own social network, dubbed "Truth Social". The platform is owned by the newly created Trump Media & Technology Group (TMTG), which also provides a video-on-demand service and "non-woke" podcasts. The following year, the takeover of Twitter by billionaire Elon Musk enabled his return to the platform, but Donald Trump declared that he preferred to communicate via his own social network.

During the campaign for the November 2022 mid-term elections, Donald Trump is intensively mobilizing his supporters at major rallies across the country. His disagreement with Florida Governor Ron DeSantis, who is presented as one of his rivals in the Republican Party, comes to public attention.

Campaign for the 2024 presidential election

On November 15, 2022, Donald Trump officially announced his candidacy for the 2024 presidential election in a speech delivered from his home in Mar-a-Lago, Florida. Among other things, he declared that "America is back" and praised the performance of his candidates in the mid-term elections, which had taken place a few days earlier.

In the weeks following the announcement of his candidacy, he resumed his rallies across the country and succeeded in collecting substantial donations. At the beginning of January 2023, a first poll showed Donald Trump winning against Joe Biden. The following March, when he became the first American president to be criminally indicted by the US justice system, some political scientists suggested that the indictment might tend to "rally more people around Trump". His popularity ratings rose sharply on the eve of his court appearance in Manhattan in April 2023.

Political positions

Donald Trump defines himself as a "conservative Republican", but commentators and opinion polls indicate that he is much less perceived as a "*true conservative*" or "*religious"* than other Republican Party figures. He says he is "totally flexible on many, many issues", and claims to be "unpredictable", which regularly leads him to change his position.

It is sometimes considered "unparalleled in American political history" or "unclassifiable".

Soufian Alsabbagh describes him as "a nativist-nationalist candidate". The historian Serge Berstein considers that he "practices populism in the same way as European populist parties"; Soufian Alsabbagh, while emphasizing his differences with the latter, believes that his electorate shares "profound motivations" with theirs. Historian Robert Paxton believes that he does not represent "right-wing extremism, but [...] extremism from the center, which advocates the supremacy of the individual". For Hadrien Desuin, Trump represents a new-generation populism: "ultraliberal in economics, he defends a strong state in the fields of defense, immigration and foreign policy".

During his 2016 election campaign, the ideas expressed by Trump and his program garnered the favor and support of ultranationalist, racist and white supremacist American far-right movements, including the Ku Klux Klan, who identify with Trump's rhetoric and see him as expressing their ideas and the American Nazi Party. For some academics like Robert Kagan and Pierre de Senarclens, he embodies a new fascism. Alain Tourigny describes him on *lenouvelliste.ca as* the unpredictable "master of the planet", with the potential to lead it into World War III. The American association Southern Poverty Law Center (SPLC), renowned for its work studying and monitoring extremist currents, considers that "Trump is a hero for the *Alt-right*", the "alternative right" grouping together different bangs of the American conservative movement sharing certain ideologies, mainly racialist or racist such as white nationalism or white supremacism, and all of which are hostile to immigration, multiculturalism and "political correctness", all themes used by Trump in his campaign.

Some analysts compare him to George Wallace, independent presidential candidate in 1968, or Andrew Jackson, seventh president of the United States. The only U.S. president to whom Donald Trump refers in his Republican Party inaugural address is Richard Nixon, through a reprise of his slogan "*Law and order", which is* seen as a significant change in a party accustomed to referring primarily to Ronald Reagan, and aims to emphasize the theme of national security. Despite often having ideas opposed to those of Ronald Reagan, the two are sometimes compared because what they have in common is that they both came from show business backgrounds, were not taken seriously by the elites and the media when they launched their bid for the White House, and were widely misunderstood when they were elected.

Conspiracy Watch sees him as a direct heir to the pseudo-conservative current analyzed by historian Richard Hofstadter in his famous lecture on the paranoid style in American politics - a right-wing extremist current that hasn't been represented at this level since Barry Goldwater's candidacy in 1964. Some observers see his propensity for lying as a manifestation of the post-truth era, in the wake of the referendum campaign on the UK's membership of the European Union; the concept of "true hyperbole", taken from his book *The Art of the Deal* (1987) and penned by his negro Tony Schwarz (en), is seen as a theorization of this technique, which he put into practice throughout his business career.

His biographers emphasize the importance in his ideological formation of Norman Vincent Peale's sermons at Marble Collegiate Church in New York, which he never stopped attending from childhood, particularly in his relationship to truth and material success.

On June 24, 2022, following the reversal of Roe v. Wade, which had guaranteed federal abortion rights for nearly half a century, Donald Trump issued a statement hailing the Supreme Court's decision as "God's will".

Privacy policy

In 1977, he married Ivana Zelníčková, a Czechoslovakian athlete and model, whom he had met in 1976 in Maxwell's Plum bar. Together they have three children: Donald Trump, Jr. (born December 31, 1977), Ivanka Trump (born October 30, 1981) and Eric Trump (born January 6, 1984). They divorced in 1992. Donald Jr, Ivanka and Eric all held positions in their father's financial empire; Ivanka and Eric later left to work in the White House.

Donald Trump denies the rumor that he had a relationship with Carla Bruni in 1991, a rumor that he himself started.

On December 21, 1993, he married actress and TV presenter Marla Maples, with whom he had a daughter, Tiffany (born October 13, 1993). The couple separated in 1997 and divorced on June 8, 1999.

Since January 22, 2005, he has been married to Melania Knauss, a model from Slovenia, with whom he has a son, Barron Trump (born March 20, 2006).

Through his son Donald, Jr. and his wife Vanessa Haydon Trump, he is grandfather to Kai Madison Trump (born May 12, 2007), Donald John Trump III (born February 18,

2009), Tristan Milos Trump (born October 2, 2011), Spencer Frederick Trump (born October 21, 2012) and Chloe Sophia Trump (born June 16, 2014). His daughter Ivanka and her husband Jared Kushner have given him three other grandchildren: Arabella Rose Kushner (born July 17, 2011), Joseph Frederick Kushner (born October 14, 2013) and Theodore James Kushner (born March 27, 2016). His son Eric and Eric's wife, Lara Yunaska, also gave him two other grandchildren: Eric "Luke" Trump (born September 2017) and Carolina Dorothy Trump (born August 2019).

Donald Trump is a Presbyterian Protestant, and claims to attend New York's Marble Collegiate Church, one of the oldest churches in the US, located in the heart of Manhattan, where he was influenced by his pastor Norman Vincent Peale, an apostle of positive thinking. Evangelical pastor Paula White is his personal spiritual advisor and has led an evangelical advisory committee to the White House.

In the culture

Highly publicized in the U.S. since the 1980s, Trump has been a fixture of American popular culture ever since.

Lise Wajeman, a professor of comparative literature, noted shortly after the 2016 presidential election that "in the space of a few months, a sort of sparse anthology of Trump avatars in series, films, comics and novels was forged on the Web", particularly among his opponents, which she believes meets "a triple necessity: to understand where the phenomenon comes from, to imagine where it's going, and to try to combat it".

In 2016 and 2017, a debate began in the United States between academics specializing in philosophy and political psychology, examining whether or not Donald Trump, who had financed his own campaign (magnificence), possesses "magnanimity" (awareness of his great possibilities), the virtue par excellence of rulers according to Aristotle: *The magnificent Mr. Trump*; *Trump's magnificence and possible magnanimity at second glance*; *Two or three things Trump should learn from Aristotle*. In this last article, Peter F. Cannavò closes the debate by pointing out that one should not confuse awareness of one's own possibly great possibilities with arrogance.

Donald Trump's plans, actions and peculiar way of expressing himself gave rise to the term "trumpisation", which in turn gave rise to "trumpiser" and "trumpisme". It was first uttered in public by former French Prime Minister Manuel Valls; this neologism was accepted by the Language Council in Sweden (trumpifiering).

In 2017, researcher Vazrick Nazari named a butterfly *Neopalpa donaldtrumpi* after Donald Trump's hair.

Fiction

In Bret Easton Ellis's novel *American Psycho* (1991), Donald Trump is cited several times by protagonist Patrick Bateman, who sees him as a role model. *In retrospect,* works of uchronic or dystopian fiction are presented as anticipations of Donald Trump's election, such as Philip Roth's *The Conspiracy Against America* (2004) or Sinclair Lewis's *It Can't Happen Here* (1935); a comparison is also made with the character of Lex Luthor, Superman's enemy elected President of the United States. In *The Parable of Talents,* a dystopian novel by Octavia E. Butler published in 1998, Senator Andrew Steele, whose supporters assemble to burn witches - which he condemns "in language so gentle that his followers were free to hear what they wanted to hear" - uses Ronald Reagan's slogan echoed by Donald Trump, "*Make America Great Again*". In 2017, Salman Rushdie's *The Golden House* mocks the president as Gary "Green" Gwynplaine.

In Hervé Le Tellier's novel *L'Anomalie* (Prix Goncourt 2020), Donald Trump is a character we guess, and has an important part in the story, although his real name is never mentioned (he is always referred to as "the American president"). He is described in the novel as bearing "a strong resemblance to a fat grouper with a blond wig".

Journalism

In January 2018, journalist Michael Wolff published the book *Fire and Fury: Trump in the White House*, which describes the first year of Trump's presidency as particularly chaotic. Testimonies reported by the author cast doubt on Trump's intellectual capacities, his ability to govern and even his mental health. The book's sales and media following reignited the debate about Donald Trump's sanity, prompting this reaction from him on Twitter: "Actually, throughout my life, my two greatest assets have been my mental stability and being, like, really smart [...]. I went from VERY successful businessman to big TV star... to President of the United States (on my first try). I guess you could call me not smart, but a genius... and a very well-rounded one at that!"

In September 2018, political journalist Bob Woodward published the book *Fear*, which describes a White House in chaos and an incompetent president overwhelmed by his task, from whom his entourage goes so far as to steal documents for him to sign to prevent him from making dangerous decisions.

Cinema

Donald Trump has made various cameos in film, mostly playing himself:

Joe Dante, director of the *Gremlins* series, drew inspiration from him to create the character Daniel Clamp in the film *Gremlins 2: The Next Generation*. Bob Gale, screenwriter of the *Back to the Future* series, says he also drew inspiration from him to imagine the character of Biff Tannen, who becomes a billionaire in an alternative future in *Back to the Future 2*. In *Wonder Woman 1984,* the role of super-villain Maxwell Lord was also inspired by Donald Trump. At the start of *Ocean's Eleven*, Danny Ocean is in Atlantic City and makes a phone call in front of a hotel owned by Trump (his name is displayed in large red neon lights).

In October 2016, during the presidential campaign, filmmaker Michael Moore released a film entitled *Michael Moore in TrumpLand* which, contrary to what the title might suggest, is not a frontal attack on Donald Trump, but a plea for Hillary Clinton. In 2018, in a documentary entitled *Fahrenheit 11/9*, he compared Donald Trump to Adolf Hitler.

He is one of the characters in the animated film *Royal Corgi* (2019).

Television

Donald Trump has made numerous cameos in television works, usually in his own role:

In 1992, in the episode *The Angel* from the series *Code Quantum*, Donald Trump as a child (played by Justin Thomson) is transported with his parents by Sam Beckett, now a cab driver. In 2000, an episode of The *Simpsons*, *The Simpsons in 30 Years*, predicted his election as President of the United States: Lisa Simpson will succeed him in 2030 after a disastrous record. Interviewed during the 2016 Republican primary campaign, screenwriter Dan Greaney says this idea "logically appeared as the last step before hitting rock bottom. It was exploited because it was consistent with the vision of an America gone mad".

On April 3, 2004, Ben Harper and Jack Johnson performed with Toots and the Maytals on Saturday Night Live (season 29, episode 16), an episode with Donald Trump as guest star.

In 2007, he was awarded the 2,327 star on the Hollywood Walk of Fame for his reality show *The Apprentice*. To denounce Trump's proposal to build a wall on the Mexican border, urban artist Plastic Jesus used the star for an ephemeral work of art, surrounding it with a wall made of wooden planks, about fifteen centimeters high and topped with barbed wire.

In season 5 of the TV series *Scandal*, the character of Hollis Doyle is inspired by Donald Trump.

His candidacy in the 2016 presidential election and his subsequent victory have made him a very recurrent character in sketches on American TV *shows. The* Saturday Night Live cartoon, starring Alec Baldwin as Donald Trump, was a big hit in the U.S. and the rest of the world, to the extent that sketches about Donald Trump and his entourage (including Kellyanne Conway, Sean Spicer, Steve Bannon and Trump's "friendly" Russian president Vladimir Putin) are among the show's top columns. Donald Trump himself has harshly criticized the show on several occasions on Twitter.

Actor Brendan Gleeson is the first actor to play Donald Trump in fiction. In September 2020, director Billy Ray adapts the memoirs of FBI director James Comey in the miniseries *The Comey Rule*.

Music

In 1990, the band The Time released a song entitled *Donald Trump (Black Version)*, written by Prince.

In 2011, American rapper Mac Miller released the track *Donald Trump*, in which he glorified the businessman's lifestyle.

On October 19, 2016, a few hours before the final televised debate between Hillary Clinton and the billionaire, rapper Eminem posted a song on his Twitter and Facebook accounts entitled *Campaign Speech*, in which he violently attacked the Republican candidate.

He is the first (and only) historical figure to be played three times in the musical clash web-series *Epic Rap Battles of History*, by Peter Shukoff in 2013 and then by Lloyd Ahlquist in 2016 and 2020.

In 2019, country singer Linda Ronstadt compares Donald Trump to Adolf Hitler.

Paint

In 1989, painter Ralph Wolfe Cowan (en) commissioned a portrait of Donald Trump; the painting was exhibited in the library of Mar-a-Lago, Donald Trump's private club in Palm Beach, Florida.

During the 2016 Republican primaries, artist Illma Gore (de) shared on a social network a portrait of Donald Trump entitled like his campaign slogan *Make America Great Again*, which depicted him naked with a micropenis, earning the artist threats of legal action from

Donald Trump's team and physical assault from a supporter of the Republican candidate. The painting was subsequently exhibited in a prestigious London gallery.

At the same time, artist Mindaugas Bonanu created a painting on the wall of a small restaurant in Vilnius, depicting a kiss between Donald Trump and Vladimir Putin, modeled on the famous kiss between Leonid Brezhnev and Erich Honecker; the work received widespread viral coverage.

Video game

In *Donald Trump's Real Estate Tycoon, an* economic simulation game of real estate speculation released in November 2002, the player's goal is to become richer than Donald Trump. Donald Trump lent his voice to both versions of the game.

In Game Developer X's *Mr. President!* game, released on Steam in October 2016, the player takes on the role of a bodyguard who must save presidential candidate Ronald Rump from multiple assassination attempts; the game occasionally parodies the themes and events of Trump's 2016 election campaign.

Comic strips

In March 2018, Éditions i published the parody album *Trump en 100 tweets,* drawn by François Boucq (Grand

Prix de la Ville d'Angoulême 1998) and scripted by Vanessa Duhamel. In 2017, cartoonist Garry Trudeau (Pulitzer Prize 1975) published a compilation of his drawings in the satirical series *Doonesbury*, in which Trump is a recurring character. In 2017, Art Spiegelman (Pulitzer Prize 1992) drew for *Resist!*, a graphic magazine in opposition to Donald Trump created by his wife Françoise Mouly and daughter Nadja.

Awards and tributes

Awards

- 1983: Tree of Life Award from the Jewish National Fund for contributions to US-Israeli relations.
- 1986: Ellis Island Medal of Honor to celebrate the values of "patriotism, tolerance, fraternity and diversity".
- 2007: Star on the Hollywood Walk of Fame.
- 2013: member of the WWE Hall of Fame.
- 2016: chosen by *Time* for its list of the 100 most influential people in the world.
- 2016: *Time* magazine's Personality of the Year, accompanied by "President of the Divided States of America".
- 2017: a Donald Trump boulevard is inaugurated in Kamza (Albania). After Donald Trump announces that the United States recognizes Jerusalem as Israel's capital, the Israeli Minister of Transport announces that the train station to be built near the Wailing Wall the following year will be named

after the American president, as will a park in the municipality of Kiryat-Yam.

Statues

After his inauguration in 2017, London's Madame Tussauds wax museum dedicated a statue to him. After his defeat in the 2020 presidential election, it is ironically updated with a version of the president in golf attire.

At the Musée Grévin, another French wax museum, a statue was unveiled on January 19, 2017, a day before his inauguration. In Berlin, the Tussaud Museum chose to represent Donald Trump's wax figure in a dumpster on November 3, 2020.

Other books by United Library

https://campsite.bio/unitedlibrary

SCAN ME

Milton Keynes UK
Ingram Content Group UK Ltd.
UKHW021838041024
449101UK00013B/845

9 789464 901764